BILLION DOLLAR PORTFOLIO

BILLION DOLLAR PORTFOLIO

HOW TO CREATE
A REAL ESTATE EMPIRE

BRENT SPRENKLE

BILLION DOLLAR PORTFOLIO
How to Create a Real Estate Empire

ISBN   978-1-5445-1764-3 *Hardcover*
      978-1-5445-1763-6 *Paperback*
      978-1-5445-1762-9 *Ebook*

CONTENTS

INTRODUCTION

Is your investment goal to own a billion dollars in commercial real estate? So why aren't you there yet? Do you know how to find properties and buy them, reposition them, raise the value, and stay competitive in an ever-changing market? If so, congratulations. If not, don't worry. If you're holding this book and willing to work hard, you are on your way to owning a billion-dollar portfolio.

Of course, there are some caveats.

Buying this book—and, of course, reading it from cover to cover—in no way guarantees that anything further will happen. The path from where you are to where you want to be is long, challenging, and requires a serious amount of work and investment. If you picked up this book thinking it's a how-to guide for getting rich overnight and buying income properties with nothing down—or some other shortcut to the world of commercial real estate—this might not be your book.

Even if you follow the advice, you are still beholden to the market and the whims of nature. That incredible rental property you found and bought for a song won't be worth as much if it's swallowed by an earthquake or burned down by looters following a riot. If the city suffers from a pandemic flu or an economic collapse, it could keep you from filling vacancies long enough to burn through your cash reserves.

Most of all, you need to be ready for the long game. Building an empire takes time, it takes patience, and it takes a massive amount of money. The allure of the endgame can sometimes blind you to these realities. If you are serious about becoming a commercial real estate mogul, if you already have a little knowledge about buying and operating property, then this book will set you on the path to success.

CAUTION VERSUS FEAR

Back in December 2007, the Great Recession began. Markets fell around the world and the prices for commercial and residential real estate dropped dramatically.

Around that time, I noticed that many real estate investors were holding onto their cash and waiting for the market to really hit what they felt was the bottom before they would start to invest in purchasing additional properties. Their logic was simple: If they waited until prices reached the absolute lowest point, they would be buying at the bottom of the market and would claim the best return on their investment with the biggest run up in appreciation.

The problem, as we will discuss many times, is that there is no defined absolute top or bottom. The market doesn't have an artificial floor or ceiling. If you decide to wait until prices hit some magic number to buy or sell, you're more likely going to miss out on many amazing opportunities.

It is the battle between caution and fear.

Caution can be an advantage. Caution makes you take stock of your assets so you know what you're able to spend and, more importantly, what you can't afford to lose. Caution pushes you to learn about the market, about the neighborhood and about the property. Cautious buyers may miss an opportunity or two, but they learn along the way. They take their losses as valuable lessons and rarely make the same mistake twice.

Fear, on the other hand, only holds you back. FOMO, or the Fear of Missing Out, may cause you to rush into acquisitions that aren't to your short- or long-term benefit. You may leap before you look, and that can be a very expensive risk. On the other side of that coin is the fear of making a mistake. If you're too afraid you won't make the purchase at all. Then you're guaranteed to completely miss out. As Wayne Gretzky once said: "You miss 100 percent of the shots you don't take."

When I spoke to commercial real estate investors in 2012, as the market started to recover from the 2008 collapse, many of them expressed regrets from being on the sideline for a few amazing years at the bottom of the market. They witnessed values appreciating and realized they'd missed that elusive "bottom." One of my clients was especially heartbroken.

He had a goal of acquiring an apartment building in a specific Los Angeles neighborhood. He knew the market, knew the industry, but he wanted to buy it at the absolute lowest point of the market. In his mind, apartment buildings sold for $200,000 per unit at the top of the market and the prices had since dropped and were trading for around $120,000 per unit, and he felt they would drop down to his target price of $100,000 per unit, so he waited, assuming he would get his way. While patiently waiting, he lined up contractors for renovations, shopped around to see which lenders were offering the most attractive financing, and figured out where he could free up liquidity for the down payment for his upcoming bargain purchases. Prices dropped slightly more and he remained on the sideline, waiting. After maybe a year went by, he looked online for the types of buildings he wanted to purchase and realized that prices were climbing. They went from $120,000 when he first started the process to $110,000 per unit and then they went straight up to $130,000 per unit with momentum behind to continue climbing.

This is where he made a common mistake. Instead of purchasing during a short-lived golden era of real estate acquisitions, he waited. In his mind, the property could still go lower in price, even though the evidence was that the market was turning around, and values were recovering. He had a number in mind and was unwilling to budge. So he waited. As values continued to soar, he completely changed his mind on attempting to purchase anything and he gave up his search, kicking himself for being too stubborn while others jumped in and took advantage of an amazing time in the market. A missed opportunity.

Many of my commercial real estate friends found themselves in similar situations. Either they waited for a type of building to hit a magical value, either a high cap rate, low cost per square foot or something similar, or they were too afraid of taking the risk on an expensive endeavor. Many were burned during the previous recession and hadn't psychologically recovered from that traumatic experience. That's one more step to overcome on the path to your billions. You have to understand the difference between caution and fear, and you need to know when you're acting with one or the other.

MEET BRENT SPRENKLE, COMMERCIAL REAL ESTATE BROKER AND INVESTOR

You have to be careful when taking someone's advice on real estate. Just because some strategy worked for them doesn't mean it will automatically work for you. While I don't consider myself the ultimate authority, I have a bit of experience on my side. I've been in this business for over twenty years, and as a commercial real estate agent I've helped sell over $1 billion in multifamily and commercial properties, consisting of over 350 transactions since I started my career. In addition, I've purchased a few dozen properties consisting of apartment buildings, industrial, hotels, and retail either on my own or with other investors.

In my time in this industry, I've seen or personally made every mistake in the book. I've bought at the top of the market, negotiated too hard on a good deal just to watch someone else buy it, and spent too much on pointless renovations. Now, I want to share that knowledge and experience with you so you can move forward with confidence—and not make the same mistakes I and so many of my clients have.

More to the point, I want to help you expand your portfolio from a small assortment of properties to $1 billion in properties.

As part of my job, I advise buyers on which properties to

buy and sell, how to reposition buildings, and how to make their money most efficiently work for them. But even the best advice doesn't work unless you're prepared. You need to come to this business with a strong work ethic and an understanding of your finances. I'm not here to help you scrape together money for your first apartment investment, but I can show you how to reposition your assets to arrange funds for your sixth.

WHY WRITE THIS BOOK?

In November 1999, faced with losing my job as an engineer building DirecTV satellites for Hughes, I was encouraged by a friend to enter the commercial real estate industry. I took a position with a regional firm as an entry-level sales broker, deciding that selling apartment buildings in Los Angeles might be a good place to begin a new career. The criteria for the job was simple: you needed a car, a computer, you had to get a real estate license, and you had to be willing to work for free in hopes that you could put some deals together to make commissions. With nothing to lose but time, I jumped in. The goal was to make great money selling buildings to and for clients but also to buy a few for myself.

What opened my eyes was the realization that there were haves and have nots in the world of commercial real estate. Investors either owned one or two buildings, or they owned dozens of them. There weren't many in the middle. Fascinated by how relatively normal people accumulated this vast wealth of commercial real estate—from apartments, to office buildings, industrial, and retail—I started asking questions. As a salesman, my job was to get to know these investors and find out what their needs were and how I could help. However, for my own personal reasons, I was truly interested in finding out how they did it, as in how they went from owning no buildings to a few to dozens and eventually to an entire empire.

There are plenty of successful individuals from real estate families that are expanding the family business, but the individuals that really intrigued me were the rags-to-riches stories: the immigrants who couldn't even speak English twenty years ago who now own half a neighborhood, or the attorney turned developer who has projects across the country, or the retired dentist who owns two hundred apartment buildings that he bought one at a time. Everyone's story is different, and they all share similar personality traits.

Having the goal of desiring to build a commercial real estate portfolio for myself, I sought out advice from these incredibly successful individuals and felt that the advice that they gave me was so important that it needed to be shared. What they told me was truly inspiring as I realized that most of these people were normal investors who worked really hard, had a plan, and executed on it. They were consistent in their work ethic, and they all had their share of struggles on their way up. Now, while I can tell people what they need to do, on a step-by-step basis, to build a billion dollar real estate portfolio, I can't make them do the hard work, nor can I help them magically find the down payment for their first deals. To get started, you'll need some form of equity, whether it's refinancing your house, selling a piece of real estate that you own, or bringing in an investor or two. The goal is for you to not only see clearly that you too can build an incredible cash-flow machine for yourself in a reasonable amount of time that will support your lifestyle and be handed on to your family but to get started today.

I completely understand that these decisions can be tricky, even for seasoned investors. That's why I didn't set out to write this book alone. I've interviewed over a dozen extremely successful and experienced investors and owners, each with massive portfolios and incredible stories, so that you can share in the wisdom of more than two hundred combined years in this business. All of these investors share one thing in common: none came from wealthy real estate families. All of them started with nothing and now hold vast and diverse real estate portfolios. You'll meet each of these real estate entrepreneurs and learn from their experience in the chapters to come.

NOT YOUR FIRST RODEO

Some of you picked up this book because you want to start

investing in commercial real estate. You've heard that income properties can be a sound investment and you want to secure your financial future with some passive income from commercial real estate. That's great. Honestly, it is a wise decision that will pay off immensely down the road but probably not immediately.

However, this is not a book to teach you how to begin. I don't want to dissuade you from learning, but I want you coming into this with your eyes open. Purchasing and renovating property is an expensive ordeal that involves an enormous amount of capital. You need to have an understanding of your finances, and the liquidity to make real changes and add real value. If you want a book about getting rich quick, this is not for you.

Some of you picked up this book because you already own a few buildings. Maybe you have a few homes that you've renovated and rented out, but now you're looking to expand into larger buildings. Perhaps you own a ten-unit apartment building or two, but now you're considering investing in something similar to a thirty-unit building. You might know people who are sitting on a hundred buildings while you struggle to find a way to purchase just a few. If any of this sounds familiar, then this book will definitely help.

If you've been in this industry for either a few weeks or decades, you also know that there is no secret formula for success. All of the tools, tips, and tricks we will cover in the coming chapters will sound familiar. What matters most is your willingness to work hard and build momentum. If you bring the drive and follow a formula, we can find your version of success.

I'll bet many of you picked up this book because you already own a few buildings and now you can't seem to find any properties for sale that seem to work for you. You don't see what you consider "good deals to buy." You constantly reminisce about the good old days when deals were cheap and readily available. But every day I look online at reports of recent commercial real estate transactions and I see great deals that just sold. Somehow or another, people out there are finding great buys. Why aren't you?

How are they doing it? Fred Leeds once told me, "You have to dig deeper," as in you have to keep calling, reading, reviewing and responding to emails, and searching online. You will expend significant effort looking for buildings to buy. A friend once told me, "You have to work really hard to find an easy deal."

WHAT ARE YOU GOING TO LEARN?

David Pourbaba shared with me what he called the "Dream of Real Estate." You buy a property, increase its value, pull all of your initial investment (the down payment) out through refinancing, and continue to own it and profit from it, to later refinance it and pull more money out and still have cash flow.

By reading this book, you'll be investing time and energy in my strategies, so what can you expect to gain? What's the return on your investment?

As I said before, this isn't a book about getting rich quickly. It's about building a proper routine that keeps you consistent so you can keep your momentum moving forward. In this business, you should always be looking for the next property to purchase, the next opportunity. On these pages, I aim to show you that there are always opportunities.

You'll learn:

- How to identify opportunities and take appropriate action.
- How to make better decisions for your properties.
- How to quit making excuses.
- How to perform risk analysis.
- How to scale your business.
- How to grow your business without giving up complete control.
- How to properly purchase properties and increase their value.

Most of all, you'll learn from real estate masters and from the mistakes and successes of your peers. You will see that there is a successful path for everyone and that you can find a simple way to achieve your goals in this industry.

You will also learn how to not be a victim of the market and make it through very tough times.

When the financial markets crashed in 2008 and then again in 2020, it caused investors to react with fear. They made decisions that ended up hurting them in the long run, either because they jumped too soon or waited too long. The truth is that there is no "perfect time" to make any financial decision. The "right" time is when you finally decide to act.

You will be able to buy buildings for what they are worth today and increase their value tomorrow. Even if the market takes a dive, even if a recession, global pandemic, or economic crisis hits, you will have increased the value of your property so that it's worth more money even in a down market than when you purchased it.

The opportunities are out there, right now, waiting for you to take action.

Are you ready?

CHAPTER 1

WHAT DO YOU WANT TO BUY?

"I bought my first building when I was twenty. It was a four-unit in El Monte. My friends at Long Beach State thought I was crazy, but I paid $45,000 for the building and thought I'd discovered electricity. The property had a 20 percent cash flow, and I sold it for a great profit just eighteen months later. I did so well and enjoyed the experience so much that I cancelled my plans to go to law school."

—RAND SPERRY

The first piece of commercial real estate I ever personally bought was a small apartment building. Nothing too fancy, just an eight-unit building in a decent Los Angeles neighborhood. It was an exciting but somewhat scary moment for me. A step into a new side of the business that I had been in for nine years already. I figured I'd make some upgrades to the building, raise the rents, and move on to then go after some much more interesting deals.

I ended up assuming a loan on the property that at the time was over 80 percent of the purchase price, which was then and still is considered incredibly high leverage. I was so excited about buying into real estate that I made two huge mistakes.

First, I bought this property at the top of the market. Now, I told you in the introduction that you can't really know when the market is at the top or bottom of its cycle. The market moves to its own beat, and anyone telling you different is trying to sell you something. In this case, I didn't do a good job analyzing my down side risk as well as the condition of the property. This was the first property I bought outside of a house and I ended up paying way more than I should.

My second mistake, and this was a big one, is the size of the loan. That leverage was way too much for the property. It would take me forever to raise the rents and have any cash flow to make this a sound investment. I was over-leveraged, which is a massive mistake in this business.

And then the market crashed.

Overnight, the property dropped in value to about the amount of the loan balance. In an instant, I had zero equity, and that left me with two choices: I could walk away or I could dig my heels in and hope for the best. This was my first foray into the world of being a commercial real estate owner, and it could not have gone much worse.

THAT GUT FEELING

"I don't like big buildings that consist of all studios or don't have parking. I call that the 'small engine effect.' It's obsolete. I prefer a building with a functional design that includes one-bedroom units, two-bedroom units, good parking, the things people need."
—BOB HART

How do you know when a property is "the one?" It's simple: Such properties don't exist.

Just like trying to time the market, there is no such thing as a perfect property. There are red flags for *bad* properties (even then, a low price will make up for just about any problems), but it can be very difficult to pick out the winners in such a crowded market. So how on Earth are you supposed to figure out what to buy?

First of all, you need to drop that mentality. If you go into this business looking for excuses not to buy, you're most likely not going to buy *anything*. There are any number of reasons to walk away from a property, but the property that you walk away from, to someone else looks like an opportunity. It's a matter of perspective, and you need to be willing to trust your abilities even more than you trust your gut.

If you own a few buildings and you want to own a few *hundred*, you can't risk losing momentum. Whether you're buying a property every year or every month, you need to set it in your mind that you are going to constantly stay active. It needs to be that simple. The most successful people in this business never stop moving forward to purchase more properties. Danny Monempour told me that there is a direct correlation between the number of offers he writes and the number of properties that he purchases. The successful investors are consistent in that they are always writing offers, touring buildings, communicating with brokers, always looking for a new property to chase, and always looking for ways to improve and add value to what they already own. That's why they're billionaires.

So how can you figure out what to buy? I made a few mistakes on my first property, but *why* did I buy it? The answer, which I regret but have to admit: I knew I'd have a small down payment, and at that time in my life, I didn't have much liquidity, and I really wanted to buy an apartment building.

I thought the building was okay, that the investment's financials were acceptable, and, as mentioned, I didn't have to come up with a big down payment. In my mind, the small down payment sealed the deal, but in hindsight that was one of the worst reasons to ever buy. Once the recession hit, the building started losing money. My rents dropped, I had vacancies, units needed renovations, and there wasn't enough income to pay the mortgage and expenses. The building was upside down, and I thought I was going to lose it. As I said earlier, I was drastically over-leveraged.

Becoming over-leveraged is when you have such a high loan on the property compared to the value of the building that there's not enough equity in it to survive a downturn. For instance, if a property is worth a million dollars—such as the building I had—and it drops in value to $800,000, and you have an $800,000 loan on it, then you have no equity. But if you have a $650,000 loan on it and it drops in value to $800,000, it should be able to weather the storm and you still have some equity in the property, which gives you a reason to fight to keep it afloat.

When you become over-leveraged, there is probably little to no cash flow. Then if a recession hits and the property drops overnight in value and the rents also substantially drop, the building is what we call "upside down," or the net income of the property is drastically lower than what it costs you to operate the building. In other words, your expenses are higher than your income and every month you are pulling cash out of your bank accounts to keep the property out of foreclosure.

That typically occurs when investors obtain loan amounts that are too large and unsustainable. Oftentimes, the people that obtain those loans do so because they don't have much available cash for a traditional down payment or they believe they can quickly raise the income. Those are the first buildings that get cratered during a recession. They typically go back to the bank as a foreclosure.

Feels like we've gone in a little circle, doesn't it? Now we're back to the billion-dollar question: How, and what, to buy?

THE CLASSIC CAR

"Early in my career, I would renovate buildings. But in recent years, I've sought out what I call "coupon clippers"—buildings that have cash flow and don't need any renovations."

—JEFF ELOWE

People are often afraid to buy investments because they are afraid that the property might drop in value. These same people are afraid to buy a stock for $10 because it might drop to $8. They consistently are missing out on the potential growth of any investment because of their fear of losing money. It's no different in real estate.

What you need to understand is there are ways to buy commercial properties where you can very quickly increase the value, so even if the real estate market drastically changes for the worse, you're prepared to weather that storm. You are basically positioning the property to be as close to recession-proof as you can by changing the economics of the building.

Buckle up, because I have an analogy for you, and we're going to get some serious mileage out of it.

I want you to imagine you found an old classic car online and you want to buy it. Sure, it's a little beat up and it needs some work, but you can see the intrinsic value. With a little elbow grease and a coat of paint, you could make that car shine, not to mention there could be a considerable profit, too.

Buildings, like classic cars, have an inherent value. If you sell the car right after you buy it, you're going to take a loss. If you spend the effort, the time and the money, you can transform that car into a real investment and it could make you a fairly hefty profit.

With my first apartment, I knew I had to put in work to receive a good return. When the market crashed, I could have walked away, taken the loss and licked my wounds, but it would have meant losing time: Time I'd already spent, and time I'd need to recoup that financial setback until I was ready for the next purchase.

Maybe you're thinking you can just simply find the property at the lowest value and set yourself up for success. I've already said that there is no real "bottom" of the market and chasing after it can be just as dangerous.

CATCHING A FALLING KNIFE

"In 2008, right when the real estate market was crashing, a friend and I bought a fourplex in Bakersfield. We got an FHA loan and put down $15,000. The price seemed really low and we felt a rural area based on agriculture and oil would come out of the recession faster than other areas. The next year, we bought fifteen more fourplexes. Within two years, we had 350 units—all in Bakersfield."

—KEITH WASSERMAN

In a down market caused by a recession, you can buy just about anything you want. It's like shooting fish in a barrel. You'll come out looking like a genius a few years later just buying any random deal that's on the market. If the market cycles are ten years, that's about three out of the ten years where you can just buy anything that fits your criteria.

Then there's typically a four- or five-year period where it's much more difficult to purchase buildings. Prices have risen and there's more competition from other buyers. That's when you have to be creative and work really hard to find even decent deals.

Maybe you don't buy twenty buildings a year during that period. Maybe you just find one a year. But as long as you keep buying and adding, that's all that matters.

There's an expression when the market is falling: You don't want to catch a falling knife. Abe Stein says a recession is like a wave in the ocean. At that moment, you should think as David Pourbaba does: "Hold on. If you can afford to, buy and hold on. No one knows where the top or bottom is."

Let's say you buy a building at the very beginning of a recession for $2 million. Your logic is that the property was previously worth $2.2 million and the 10 percent discount is appealing enough for you to move forward. However, the market might continue to drop and about a year later it's now worth $1.6 to $1.8 million. You probably would have been better off at the beginning of the recession to wait for the market to shake out. Rents almost always drop during recessions, which negatively impacts values. Maybe there is a one- or two-year period where the market is correcting and you take a more reactive "wait and see" approach, but that in my opinion is the only time where you're not aggressively seeking buildings to purchase. That's just because the market's dropping and you just don't know when it's going to stop. Purchasing during this period is what we refer to as "trying to catch a falling knife."

The real question is: When have values dropped enough

that you can once again start to buy? The simple answer is, "When the deals make sense," as in when you can purchase a building and feel comfortable that the rents are not going to drop, obtain an attractive loan with a reasonable down payment, and have the building actually make money for you the day you close escrow. That's when you buy. You don't worry about whether it's going to drop a little bit more in value. It might, and it doesn't matter, as this is a long-term business. If it goes from $2 million to $1.8 million and then straight up to $2.5 million, I'd say that was a colossal home run.

What you also need to focus on is *adding value* to the property.

A COAT OF PAINT AND NEW CARPETS

"I believe in 'value add to the max' when renovating properties. I understand the need to make sure the roof and plumbing are all in good repair, but those features don't make the building worth more; buyers expect those features to work well. However, upgrading the cosmetics and interiors are what make a building worth more money."

—JERRY FINK

If you take a classic car that is worth $10,000 and add a brand-new interior, you've slightly increased the overall value of the car (unless you're trying to sell to a purist, as they won't appreciate you "modernizing" the vehicle).

You would expect that the next buyer would factor that into their estimated price. That same concept works with your properties.

The most common and obvious way to add value to a property is just increasing the rents.

Sometimes, it's as easy as buying a building and just giving everybody a rent increase. That's the oldest and easiest trick in the book. It's properly researching the rental market, comparing the units at the property that you are purchasing with other apartments for rent in the surrounding area and making a sound business decision. Is there immediate upside in the rents that you can tap into?

As an example, you are considering buying a building and you think that the apartments are worth $1,250 per month in rent. Maybe you're not sure, so you look at comparable buildings in the neighborhood and see what they are asking for rent. Your tenants are paying $1,000, which means you have some room to move the rents up. However, you don't make any money with an empty building, you don't have the budget to renovate the units, and you are aware that none of your tenants will actually *enjoy* having their rent drastically increased. So how should you navigate that?

You could potentially raise all of the existing tenant's rent from $1,000 to $1,150. Your tenants will most likely consider moving elsewhere until they realize that everything for rent in the area is at $1,250, so if they're paying $1,150, they're still at a discount. Some of the tenants will leave as they can't afford it. The rest will most likely stay.

There are no hard feelings here. You have to make business decisions that are in your best interest, and they need to make sure their budgets don't get overwhelmed. It's a mutual relationship, so you're offering them a deal.

Those units that move out, you remodel them as best you can within your budget, then you rent them out for $1,250 monthly. Now all of a sudden, you have a third of the units paying $1,250 and the rest of the units paying $1,150. You've increased an average rent to around $1,200, which is 20 percent higher than when you bought it, but you've increased the net income almost 35 percent as the expenses aren't that much different now.

The expenses aren't drastically different because you only renovated where you needed to, and you haven't made drastic changes to the property otherwise. You have the same utilities, mortgage, insurance, trash removal, gardening, and cleaning bills. Therefore, the net income is 35 percent higher, which increases the value of the property by about 30 percent. All you had to do was raise the rents 15 percent to 20 percent and you just increased the value of the property by 30 percent. Even in the worst recession, properties rarely drop more than 30 percent. You could have bought the building at the top of the market, had the market correct and drop, and come out of it just fine.

That's just from a relatively modest rent increase.

The second straightforward way to add value is finding other ways to generate income: You can add a laundry room; you start charging for parking; you start charging tenants for late fees and storage, small things of that nature.

Maybe you find tenants who have pets or more occupants in the unit than they should have on the lease. (The lease says no pets and they decided they wanted a cat and a dog, or they're supposed to have two occupants and it turns out they have four). Then you renegotiate their rent and the tenants are probably happy to pay it because it would be a big pain in the neck to move just because they have a dog there or are four people in one apartment.

Perhaps you own a retail property with a triple net lease that allows you to charge the tenants for insurance and property taxes, but you haven't been. You could simply enforce your lease and require them to pay what they are obligated to.

No matter how you approach your business of adding value, you need to have a plan. It is critical that you have a specific business plan for each property that you buy, and annually you should re-examine each property to determine what you can do to add value.

Very few people buy a commercial property and simply turn it over to property management and tell them to do absolutely nothing beyond collecting rents and paying bills. Most people purchase buildings and have very specific goals in mind to add value to the property, such as raising rents, adding additional amenities, or finding additional revenue streams. However, most people, within a year, completely forget about the property. This is a mistake as management doesn't have the interest or the capacity to continue pushing on your added-value plan to improve the property. You need to keep on top of it.

That essentially is the basics of a business plan. You look at your assets, see how you can leverage them for greater value, and find the steps you need to take in order to make that happen. If you bought that classic car with the intention to sell it for a profit, you need to plan out how you're going to renovate it before you put it on the market for sale.

When investors set out to acquire commercial real estate, it's best to have a predetermined business plan on how they are going to purchase the property, reposition it, and sell or refinance the asset for a healthy profit so they can move on to the next property. Since you are now holding this book, I know that last point really sticks out. It's not enough to work on one building forever. We have to reach for the next one.

Everyone brings a different plan to real estate investment. David Pourbaba looks to buy in good neighborhoods and typically never sell—which is his "law of real estate." Danny Monempour looks at the gross rent multiplier (GRM), cap rate, and cost per square foot on the properties that he is looking to purchase, then compares these three factors to other properties for sale. If one is an outlier in a positive way, that encourages him to purchase the property. If one is an outlier in a negative way, he will pass on the opportunity. Paul Ling seeks to purchase buildings that have a very low cost per square foot. Not on the land cost but on the existing building. The reason is because of depreciation, and a larger building structure gives you more property to depreciate, creating a larger tax write-off.

Wow, we keep bringing it back to that first question! How do you decide what to buy? Well, I finally have an answer for you: It depends on your business plan.

PLANNING TO BUY

"The City of Lakewood, a planned community near Long Beach that was developed after World War II, had some land leftover after its booming development of the 1950s. As I did previously in Inglewood, I developed the strategy for acquiring the land

and developing it, and my partners put up the money. We built a HUD housing development on the site, and then a few years later built fifty condos on the remaining land."

—THOMAS SAFRAN

Every business needs a plan. I know that may sound reductive, but you'd be surprised how many people get themselves into serious financial trouble by going with their "gut" rather than a solid and realistic plan. Real estate is no different. If you want to be successful, if you want to own large properties and work toward that "billion-dollar portfolio," you need a plan of attack.

First, you need to have a look at your liquid assets. How much capital do you have at your disposal? Commercial real estate is always expensive, whether small or large. Do you have the cash on hand to make a large down payment (don't forget what happened to me when I took on a high leverage loan)?

Second, with the money you have on hand, how much are you willing (and able) to put into your next purchase? Everyone needs to keep some cash reserves available for a rainy day—a slush fund to make repairs, upgrades, and to spend adding value to a property. Make sure you aren't sitting on too much, though. Paul Ling says, "Keeping money in the bank earning almost 0 percent is the worst thing you can do."

If you are buying a building that needs to be renovated and the down payment is $1 million, you have to be able to absorb that investment and still have funds available for upgrades and repairs. You probably need an additional 10 percent of the purchase price available on top of the money you need for the down payment. A fatal flaw that investors often make is that they buy buildings and don't have any funds left to make improvements or repairs afterwards. They assume that the building will generate enough cash flow to allow them to make repairs and upgrades without having to come out of pocket, and rarely does that work out as planned.

When you're looking at the market for your next purchase, you may want to direct your attention to buildings that are "heavily devalued." Those properties can provide the best bang for your buck. What is a heavily devalued building?

There are a number of factors that can make a property heavily devalued:

- The rents are drastically below market, and typically it's because of the condition of the property.
- The current owner has held the property for over ten years and has a very small loan on it. Most likely, they are unmotivated to push the property hard.
- The current owner lives out of town and has turned it over to unmotivated management.

- All the expenses are just unbelievably high. As an example, the prior year's utilities and repairs were 25 percent to 50 percent more than what a normal building should be.
- The current owner failed to push rents and make substantial renovations when units became vacant.
- The current owner failed to try to minimize recurring expenses.
- The current owner failed to make any meaningful long-term improvements to the building, which would increase the net income to the property.
- When units, either apartments, office, or retail, become vacant, the current owner just elects for "paint and carpet" to turn the vacancies instead of a full gut remodel.
- The façade and landscaping haven't been touched in decades, which impacts leasing.

The pros of buying a heavily devalued property are simple enough: It's probably not going to get much worse than what it is currently. You can raise the rents and increase the value of the property as they are at the bottom of the rental market to begin with. If a standard property can be increased 10 to 20 percent, a heavily devalued one could go as high as 40 percent.

If you buy a building for $1 million and afterwards increase its value 40 percent to $1.4 million, in theory you can then buy another building for $10 million and increase the value to $14 million. That's called wealth generation. It's the goal of this entire book.

The downside to it, the reason the property is neglected, is most likely that the building is a pain in the neck to the current owner. There's a reason why the rents are low. There's a reason why the expenses are high. The building is probably very challenging to manage. There is inherent risk here, and many people don't want to take that on. They don't want to buy a building that needs too much heavy lifting. They want it to be easy.

For some investors, these disadvantages are a small price for a great turnaround. For others, these red flags halt the sale. For Abe Stein, it's when the rents are unstable or above market. He'd rather buy properties with lower rents to avoid vacancies as well as having long-term upside. Jeff Elowe avoids properties with questionable construction elements or deep environmental concerns, as these are issues that can't be quickly and inexpensively corrected—and when they go to sell the property, it will also be an issue for the next buyer.

Let's rip off the Band-Aid right now. Buying commercial real estate is not the easiest thing to do. It takes hard work, self-motivation, and understanding the Three T's: Tenants, Trash, and Toilets (more on this later). Buying heavily devalued buildings and putting in all the work necessary for wealth generation takes a particular kind of person. If you're reading this book, that might just be you.

So with these types of buildings, you need to have reasonable expectations. Understand that there's a reason why it's devalued. It's because it's going to be more work than something else. It's what we call a *non-performing asset*. To me, I see it as a *value-added* opportunity.

It's like that beat-up old car we mentioned earlier. You buy the car and figure out how to get the most bang for the buck out of it, but not all improvements are equal. If you paint the car, is it going to be worth much more than what you paid for it? If you fix the engine, it's worth more. If you add a pair of fuzzy dice, you're not really changing much.

Same thing with an apartment building. If you buy an apartment building that has a bad roof, adding a $20,000 roof is not going to increase the value of the property by $30,000, let alone the $20,000 that you just spent on it. People expect the roof to be in good condition. If you're buying a building that needs a $20,000 roof, you and the seller need to work that one out. Otherwise, you're eating that cost without getting the full value of that investment.

Bob Hart has what he calls his "three-pronged approach" for renovations and building upgrades. This includes deferred maintenance, amenitization—or refreshment of amenities—and then an ongoing unit renovation program. But as far as mechanical systems are concerned, Bob believes that "no one pays you for infrastructure," so it's important to not purchase properties with plumbing issues and other basic services not being functional.

What you have to focus on is buying buildings where you can make small, incremental improvements to the property that result in substantial increases in value, such as cosmetic upgrades. Paint and landscaping don't cost much money. If you can change the physical appearance of a property, you can probably generate drastically higher rents. The same thing is true of the interior. If the office space, retail space, and apartments are in terrible condition, you're not going to collect very good rents from them and definitely not high-quality tenants. If you can buy a property with unattractive units and make reasonably priced upgrades to them, you will then be able to charge higher rents and recoup your investment quickly.

SOURCING PROPERTIES AND DEAL FLOW

One of the critical aspects that separates those who own five buildings from those who own fifty is what we refer to as having consistent "deal flow." **Deal flow** is the constant sourcing of new properties that may potentially work for your investment criteria. Successful owners are constantly underwriting new properties and making offers, oftentimes with a low success rate. However, even if you write offers on one hundred properties a year and land five of them, which is only 5 percent, you've still managed to purchase five properties in a year. That is quite remarkable for something that should only take a few hours a day once you have your process streamlined. As Bob Hart once said to me, "If you hang around the basket long enough, eventually you'll catch a rebound."

The one thing you need to understand with commercial real estate, unlike single family, is that there is no particular place on the internet where everything is advertised for sale. Probably half of the properties that sell are never actually advertised, as in they never hit the broad market. Either a seller and buyer cut a deal direct, or a broker just brings an owner an offer that they are willing to accept. So it's important that you don't expect to find every deal just sitting there on the internet, waiting for you to finally get around to calling the listing agent.

You will need to create a daily habit of searching to see what came up for sale, what had a price reduction, what fell out of escrow that you were considering previously, and lastly tracking what has sold. With this knowledge, you are educating yourself on the market, the competition, and the sales professionals that you need to network with.

Rao Yalamanchili once told me that he quickly reviews around five hundred emails every day at six o'clock in the morning, just looking for what in his mind is worth pursuing. Then he contacts the agent, obtains the marketing info, puts the data into their model, and determines whether or not it fits his criteria and is worthy of an offer. This is a very efficient system and no doubt is one of the reasons behind Rao's amazing success. In one word, it's consistency.

HOW TO SOURCE POTENTIAL DEALS

Directly Contact Brokers: This is the easiest way to get started. Go on the internet and see what is for sale in the product type that you want to purchase. Loopnet.com, Costar.com, your local multiple listing service (MLS), your local newspaper, commercial real estate publication, or other various websites. Every area has different publications and websites, and everyone will have different properties advertised for sale. Networking events are a great way to meet hungry brokers who might be able to source some deals for you. Essentially, you need to be contacting the listing agents to obtain info on the properties that you want to buy. It's important for you to not only be respectful to these agents but to become friendly with them, as when a great deal comes up they can call *anyone* to sell a great deal, and you want to be the one that receives that phone call.

Danny Monempour, one of the friendliest and most successful owners that I deal with, takes and returns every phone call. He once told me that you never know where a deal might come from, so you need to speak with everyone. He also hosts annual holiday parties and invites all of the brokers. The results speak for themselves: He receives more deal flow than probably anyone, which has allowed him incredible opportunities. Once these brokers see that you are serious, they will start calling you when properties come up, which is the situation that you want to be in. Ask Danny!

Tracking: Some owners have a very specific criteria of properties that they want to purchase. Whether it's big box drug stores (CVS or Walgreens) in the southeast, high rise office buildings in Seattle, or twenty- to forty-unit apartment buildings built in the 1980s in the Bay Area, these owners track everything that comes on the market or is in play that fits their criteria. They contact the listing agent, let them know what they would pay by preferably giving them an offer, and they consistently follow up with the listing agents every few weeks to see what is going on. Four things will happen to each property:

1. It will sell to someone else at a higher price than what you will pay.
2. It will go into escrow with someone else and then fall out and become available again.

3. It will sit on the market until the listing expires and the owner takes it off.
4. There will be a price reduction, and then maybe it will sell.

Regardless of what happens, following the type of property and individual properties that you want to purchase will greatly educate you on the values of these properties as well as what your competition will pay. This will also allow you to make a few purchases and establish a great relationship with the deal-making brokers that specialize in them. You will notice that a handful of brokers will dominate each product type in each market and you need to become very friendly with them. Be patient and be prepared to *not* buy the property. Someone else probably will eventually, and you might not get your price.

Direct Contact: This might come as a surprise, but often we receive direct mail from prospective buyers that are interested in either a specific property we own, or they are just fishing by sending mail or text messages to a general mailing list that they paid for. For instance, I receive in the mail letters saying, "Hi, I want to buy your commercial property and I'm a local owner." I've been told that these strategies often work coming out of a recession, but once multiple people start a similar mailing strategy, the results fade. A title company can set you up with this mailing list and you can hire a company to send the mail out, often a local postcard or mailing company. But you'll need to be specific in mailing letters to owners of a certain property type and neighborhood, size of building, vintage, etc. Let them know that you are a principal, not a broker, and that you want to buy their property.

Lately I've been receiving text messages from random people. This one just came in: "Hello, Brent Sprenkle, I'm from Warwick Investment and we're looking to see if your property on Westmoreland Ave. is up for sale. Let us make you an offer." Where they received my name, phone number, and building address is a mystery, but I'm willing to bet that they send hundreds of these out a day through a relatively simple electronic system. Yesterday I received an anonymous text from someone saying, "Hi, I know we are in a really challenging time right now. I hope this message finds you well. We're just reaching out to let you know that we are interested in making you a cash offer for your property. Let me know if you are interested in selling. Thank you and be safe." What kind of results these people get is unknown, but if they get one deal out of it, it's worth it.

Broker Network: Besides calling brokers that have properties for sale that you are interested in purchasing, you can also look to see what has sold in the particular type of property and neighborhood that you are interested in. Call the brokers involved and let them know that you would have bought those properties and you are interested in similar deals. Periodically contact these brokers. While it's not always easy to find them, if you are willing to pay for services like Costar you can obtain the contact information. A title company can also help you. Getting to know twenty-five to fifty brokers that specialize in the type of property you are interested in will allow you to obtain access to most of the properties that become available. This is a relationship business.

Bargain Hunting: While most buyers are interested in one particular property type—such as twenty to thirty-unit apartment buildings in one zip code or mid-rise office buildings in another particular submarket—there exists a type of buyer who buys just about everything on arbitrage. This buyer knows that apartment buildings in a certain area sell for $200,000 per unit, so when something shows up at $150,000 per unit, he or she takes a run at it. Or if office buildings sell typically for $100 per square foot in an area and something hits the market at $70, it's time to make a phone call.

These buyers, being opportunists, typically purchase everything from office, retail, industrial, land, apartments, and even single-family homes. More interestingly, they are open to various markets. These are the real entrepreneurs of our business. They track anything that's a bargain. Even if they buy a property that doesn't necessarily work out, the logic is that they purchased the property at such a low value compared to the market that someone else will be willing to pay more for it shortly afterwards, provided economic conditions remain the same or improve.

Big Game Hunting: This is the tracking of a specific large property. Real Estate Investment Trusts (REITs) and other institutions typically dominate the space of one-hundred-plus unit Class A apartment buildings and $50 million plus Class A commercial properties, and the question arises of whether or not you want to compete with institutional buyers. They certainly have more resources behind them, both financially, strategically, and staffing.

The logic is that large properties create an excellent economy of scale, as their large size creates efficiencies in financing, investors, and management. But that same scale also equates to drastically larger downside risk. Some buyers target purchasing large assets that are undermanaged and need renovations. They will reposition these properties in hopes of taking it from Class B to Class A, with the idea that they will later sell the property to an institutional investor (who historically pay more than private capital investors), and if they can't execute a sale, they have the option of refinancing the property, recapitalizing the asset, or some other creative strategy.

In general, it's much harder to find a bargain on the larger properties, as there are less of them to go around, and the owners (both the buyers and seller) are typically more sophisticated with greater resources, and the properties tend to be better managed with less upside, but opportunities always exist. The market is efficient but not perfect, and owners fall asleep behind the wheel, allowing management to run it into the ground more often than you would like to believe.

Clustering of Properties: When your home market becomes overheated and you need to head out of town to find properties that work, it's important to not just purchase one building in an area far from home, as it's both inefficient and impractical. Bob Hart once told me that they like to cluster properties, as in purchasing multiple properties all in one market—and a short drive from each other. When they fly out to visit their properties, they can see all of them in a matter of a few hours, as well as a few that they are interested in acquiring, which makes it much more efficient for their operations. It also allows them to create a presence in that particular market so that when properties come up for sale, they receive the first phone call from the listing agent.

Neighborhood Speculations: Essentially, this is tracking everything that comes on the market in a particular neighborhood. About fifteen years ago, there was an investor who became fascinated with a small and overlooked neighborhood in Los Angeles called San Pedro. He would buy anything in that market—small and large apartments, retail, office; you name it, he would buy it if he could make the deal work. He felt that the area was up and coming, and he was right. The area gentrified and those properties rapidly appreciated.

If you think you found the next A quality neighborhood at B or C quality pricing, and you are willing to speculate and be patient, this approach has worked well in the past—but it's also backfired. When the economy and rental market turns, these transitioning areas often are devastated and wipe the owners out, so please make sure that the fundamentals are healthy for each property that you are purchasing, as in the properties actually make money and your investment isn't 100 percent predicated on future growth and potential income. The upside is great, but it doesn't pay your bills today. Buying a dilapidated retail strip center could be a great opportunity until a few years later a Walmart or Target opens a mile down the street and suddenly you have no tenants. You must be careful and find out what's being planned in the area.

A Fickle Criteria: Create a very specific criteria of what works for you. From the size of the property, to the neighborhood, vintage, number of units, leasable square footage, parking, amenities, etc. Then target everything that fits that criteria and let the listing agents know of not only your detailed interest but what you will pay. Then *follow up repeatedly*. Again, be prepared to not land many deals when your criteria is very particular, but as long as you keep searching and making offers, eventually you will land something. Maybe you only land one property in a particular year, but the next year you land five. And all six of these were amazing deals that you can immediately resell for a profit or refinance your down payment out. Sometimes, being picky and patient as well as being willing to grow slowly is the way to go.

A mass email recently went out from a buyer; it provided not only specific criteria, but also information on his formulaic approach to buying. His goal was to always be north of a 5 percent cap rate, so he used this simple formula:

SGI x 55 percent = NOI / Sale Price Must Be At Least a 5 percent CAP

This investor's criteria was that the Scheduled Gross Income (SGI) with 45 percent removed for operating expenses is the Net Operating Income (NOI). The NOI divided by the purchase price for this buyer must be at least a 5 percent Cap Rate. While this is a very simplistic way to calculate your purchase criteria, you can see just how clear and focused this buyer was on meeting a specific threshold. If the scheduled income of a property he is considering is $200,000, he assumes the NOI is $110,000 by multiplying by 0.55. If he then divides this theoretical $110,000 NOI by the asking price of $2.2 million, it's a 5 percent cap rate for him, which meets his criteria.

Finally, don't be stubborn when you find a property you absolutely want to buy. I've seen many people walk away from a great deal because the asking price was one or two percent higher than they'd wanted. If the value will appreciate potentially 10 percent a year, every month the property is worth close to 1 percent more. By the time a typical two-month escrow closes, the property that you felt you were overpaying 2 percent for has appreciated 2 percent and you've paid market or potentially even less. Over time, even with modest appreciation, everything goes up in value. Remember, a rising tide lifts all boats.

Develop your own strategy—whether it's tracking properties you are interested in, following up with ten local brokers, or targeting a specific neighborhood, you will need to determine what works best for you, and don't be afraid to mix your business plan up as the market evolves and your criteria changes. You always need to be nimble and evolve as the investment market progresses.

TWO PATHS AHEAD

"In the 1980s, when interest rates skyrocketed and the country fell into a recession, I was forced to sell my entire collection of artwork to pay my bills. I regret that decision. I also failed to be as aggressive as I should have been at times."

—ABRAHAM STEIN

The main lesson that I want to share is that all things will pass. All problems will eventually be worked through. All down markets will eventually come back up. All recessions will eventually end. The investors who are the most successful are the people that quit making excuses. In a recession, the reason why there's no longer people that are buying is that 90 percent of the people are too scared or have too many excuses.

Ten percent of the investors, during a market collapse, will look at the current situation and think to themselves, "This is a great opportunity. These buildings are valued much lower than they were two years ago. I think I want to buy several. I'm sure eventually the tenants will come back and I'm sure eventually the problems that we're having in the economy will end. At that point, these buildings will be worth what they were worth a couple years ago at the top of the market, but I will have bought them for less and I'm going to feel like a genius."

Those are the people who always end up being extremely wealthy and successful, because they were the ones that were willing to not get caught up in the depressing behavior that so many people exhibited.

I remember in 2011, and again in 2020, just turning the news on the radio off. I couldn't stand driving to work and hearing nothing but one story after another about people losing their jobs, about people losing their houses, about companies going out of business. I didn't even want to hear the news, because it was so negative. If I listened to all the things they said, I might as well have just turned around and gone right back home and not even gone to work. It was so negative.

Immediately after I bought my first apartment building, the market crashed and all of the money that I invested was, on paper at least, wiped out at that moment. I had two options: hang on or walk away. Thankfully, I had enough of a head on my shoulders to think past the next few months.

Right now, if you're reading this in 2021 or afterwards, many of you are in a similar boat. Who could have predicted a global pandemic? That doesn't mean you're out of options. There are always choices to make, and there is always a way forward. Believe me, a market crash hurts. I'm here to tell you that I survived and so will you. As Bob Hart says, "If you only see the way up, you will get stung, and the best offense in real estate is a good defense."

As I've said, the market is cyclical. If you wait long enough, it will turn for the better. I decided to wait.

It wasn't easy. Money wasn't exactly pouring in during the recession. At one point, I even called the lender to let them know I was having trouble. Wasn't that a fun conversation?

Me sitting there, metaphorically hat in hand, asking what they can do to help me out? I wanted them to reduce the interest rate, but they wouldn't. I tried every trick I knew, but it wasn't enough. At the end of the day, I just decided I was going to have to hold on and suffer through it and hope for the best.

I didn't walk away. Recently, for the purposes of a cash-out refinance, I had that property appraised for double what I paid for it. Even though I almost lost it in foreclosure, that property has stuck with me, just as I stuck by it.

And with that refinance money now in my bank account, I can start to look at the next property to buy.

CHAPTER 2

CASH AND EQUITY

"My family owned a small amount of real estate when I was young, but my dad died when I was in my twenties and I was bought out from the family textile business by the time I was twenty-two. Leaving the family business this way was not an enjoyable experience, but eventually I saw more of a future in the real estate business. About two years after I was bought out, I met a man named Arthur Kaplan, who was in the pickle business. We founded a construction company and called it KB Construction. We specialized in office buildings. Over the next twenty-five years, we built around fifty office buildings in Los Angeles."

—STANLEY BLACK

One of the biggest issues investors in this business face is selling their properties. They're so focused on achieving the highest possible sale price that they end up missing out on an opportunity. What you have to realize is there is no *best* time or *highest* price to sell. There is no magic number that equals the highest value of the property. You should sell when the price is equal to the opportunity.

I had a client named James who was struggling with selling a property. He'd been toying with the idea of unloading a building for some time but could never pull the trigger. We would list it for sale, receive offers, and then he would ultimately change his mind on selling. The price just wasn't high enough in his mind, and he couldn't get comfortable with the buildings that would be available for him to purchase afterwards.

Finally, I asked him what it was that he wanted. If we couldn't agree on this step, maybe we could start on the next one and work backwards. So I asked what property he was looking to buy. What kind of cash did he need to make this deal? James told me he wanted to buy a larger apartment building in downtown Los Angeles, something that was rundown and in need of renovation. He'd actually found his ideal property on his own, but he didn't know what to do with the first building.

At this point, I'd listed James's original property enough times that I had a buyer lined up for it, someone who we could count on to close a transaction and was also willing to pay what we felt was the fair market value. Now we knew what we wanted to buy, and the general amount we were about to make from the sale. I went to the owner of the larger apartment building in downtown LA and negotiated the deal. The seller was willing to work with us on a timetable that allowed James to sell his property, free up the down payment, and come into this new building with reserves for the project ahead.

James had been hesitant to take any steps forward with his first property. We'd gone to market time and again, but he wanted to wait for the "perfect price and opportunity." It was only when we decided how we wanted to use that equity that he was able to take action and make the sale. Now he has the type of building that he always wanted to own, and he's still looking toward the future and his next move.

In our last chapter, we realized that we needed a solid business plan in order to select the right building for our next purchase. Before you act on that plan, however, you need to have the money ready, and know how to make it work for you. It's not enough just to have cash. You have to understand the value it brings in this business. As Paul Ling once told me, "No matter how smart you are, without capital, you can't get anywhere."

For this chapter, you need to look at your assets. What is your financial situation, and how are you going to find the funds you need for that next purchase?

MANAGING YOUR GREED

"Most people don't know how to manage their greed. They won't allow themselves to realize when you should take a profit. If you buy something for a million dollars and a year later it's worth two million, you have to manage your greed and say, 'That's a huge profit. I'm going to take the money and run.'"

—ANDREW TAVAKOLI

A client of mine named Andrew once mentioned this expression "managing your greed." At first, I was startled by the phrase. I don't think of this work as greedy, and I certainly wouldn't want to accuse anyone of such. After talking for a few minutes, he clarified.

Imagine you purchased a building for $1 million, and your expectations were to sell the property once the value climbs to around $1.5 million. When you are ready to sell, you are pleased to find out that the property is actually worth $1.6 million. Now, instead of selling as you intended, you start to think that you can wait and find someone to pay $1.7 million or more. You keep the property on the market at an aggressive price, letting the listing become stale. As an investor, you did a poor job of managing your greed. You're stepping over a dollar to pick up a dime.

When we're talking about this particular market, the numbers grow very high very quickly. It's easy for newer buyers to experience sticker shock, especially if you're moving into a market like Los Angeles for the first time. In the same way, it's easy to look at how much these buildings sell for and get a little over eager with your own property. Just like James, you need to understand that there is no perfect time to sell. Your building doesn't have a magic number that equals its highest ever value. The right time to go into escrow is when the profit from the sale matches the equity necessary for your next move. You need to be smart and have a plan. You need to manage your greed.

A client of mine approached me in 2005 about selling an apartment building. Let's call him Bob. I evaluated the property at $2 million, which was a great profit from his original investment. He then said, "You know what? I think I need to further renovate the property. I have a unit that is going to move out. If I renovate that unit and get a higher rent, I think I can push the property to $2.1 million in value."

I said, "Okay, but you know you're going to have to spend money on that. It's going to take some time, and then whatever else you buy at that point in an exchange is going to be more expensive."

Bob said, "I'm willing to take that chance."

A year later, the tenant in the apartment he wanted to renovate moved out, and my client contacted me to sell the building. I said, "Congratulations, upon our review we believe that it's actually worth about $2.15 million now."

Bob said, "You know what? All my units are going to have their annual 3 percent rent increase in about four months. Once that happens, I think the building is worth $2.2 million. Let's talk then."

Four months later, I sat down with him and delivered positive news, "Guess what? You've raised the rent, but the market has also improved. It's worth $2.25 million now."

Now, Bob's becoming really excited and says, "You know, a friend of mine thinks I can install a rooftop deck and that would be a great amenity, and I should then be able to achieve a higher rent and the building will be worth more."

I tried to reason with him. "Well, your existing tenants are not going to pay more in rent for that. It's a rent-controlled building. But if that's what you want to do, that's your decision."

Six months later (this was around 2007), I followed up with him and he was working with the city to get the roof deck approved. Six months later, he finally had it approved, and another six months later, it was done. He wanted to meet and I delivered the following news to him, "Okay, now it's 2009, and the real estate market has just crashed. We could have sold it for $2.25 million a year ago. You were hoping to get to $2.4 million. It's probably worth $1.9 million now."

Bob hesitated and then commented, "I guess I should have taken your advice and sold the property at $2.25 million, but I was just too greedy."

Again, I don't want you to think of "greed" as a vicious, sinful thing in this business. My client had an investment, and he was trying to make it as valuable as possible. He saw an opportunity that he felt he could increase the value of the property a little bit more. In fact, he did increase the building a little bit more in value, but the market crashed on him. He was trying to get the last drop of value out of that building.

You can't always control external forces such as the market, the economy, a looming recession, or a terrorist attack. That was his problem. He couldn't set a reasonable expectation of when to sell. He had to take every last nickel of value out of the property. He had to squeeze every last drop of juice out of that lemon. He wound up selling the property for about two million dollars, but that was six years after I told him he could sell it for two and a quarter million.

It's not just about the money he lost, but the time and effort that he spent. Had he not been so focused on another 5 percent, he could have moved on to the next deal such as buying at the bottom of the market. You can't have the blinders on in this business, you can't be too precious with your assets and you can't get caught up emotionally. Once you've turned enough of a profit that you can afford the next building, it's time to move on. If you want to build that billion-dollar portfolio, you can't be upset over losing out on that last small percentage that's going to be nearly impossible to achieve.

KNOWING WHEN TO MAKE YOUR MOVE

"I was studying microbiology at UCLA and planning to become a doctor when my uncle lured me into the property management business. I collected rent for him, helped tenants with minor requests, and did small repairs. Eventually, my uncle sent me to Houston to buy office buildings, and I began investing with him and taking more of an ownership position in the properties."

—DAVID SOUFER

There is an expression: You need to leave a little bit of meat on the bone for the next buyer. If your goal is to add value to a property and later sell it, you can't spend every last cent turning the building into a piece of art.

Think about our first chapter, when we had to decide what building to buy. If you were looking on the market at what's available and you had two compelling choices, would you go with: A) a thirty-unit building that has rents at full market level with every known amenity, or B) a thirty-unit heavily devalued building where the tenants are paying 20 percent below market on rent? In one case, you stand to take on a small loan and potentially add an immense amount of value. In the other case, you're buying a property with little to improve and you'll be subject to what the market brings.

Some people will buy a building, and let's just say it's a thirty-unit apartment building, and they'll renovate ten units. Twenty other units haven't been renovated. Of the ten units that they've renovated, they collect top rent for those units and then they either sell the building or refinance it and move on to the next property.

Those people always perform amazingly well. They make a quick profit and either refinance and leave a fair amount of meat on the bone for themselves, or they sell and leave more potential growth for the next buyer. That's a low-risk investment.

Then there are other people like Bob who just can't help themselves. They want to get every single tenant out of the building, renovate every unit, get the top possible rent, and push the rent as high as they possibly can. When they go to sell that building, no one else wants to buy it. They look at it and think, "How am I going to do better than what the current owner did? There's nothing left for me to improve."

It's the ultimate example of not being able to manage your greed by setting a realistic expectation of when to consummate a deal and take an enormous profit. You see the same thing with stocks.

In 2000, when I first entered into the real estate business, there was a guy in my office named Dan. He had a family friend who was working for a small tech startup that specialized in business-to-business software. They had a stock IPO and Dan bought a bunch of their stock for something like five dollars a share.

Shortly afterwards, the stock went to $25 based on expectations of their software that wasn't even developed yet. At this time Dan had the ability to sell his shares and make roughly a $200,000 profit, which for someone in their 20's in 2000 was a huge amount of money. There was an apartment building that Dan was in escrow to purchase, and the down payment for the property that the lender was going to require was about $250,000.

He didn't have much cash in the bank and he was going to simply sell the stock for the down payment. At this point, the stock was worth about $300,000. I mentioned to Dan, "Man, you should just sell the stock, because you're going to have $300,000, your down payment is $250,000, and you'll still have $50,000 left to make some improvements or maybe pay some taxes."

Dan replied, "No. I'm going to sell the stock right before the close of escrow because I bet it'll be worth $350,000 by then. It just keeps going up." A couple weeks later, Dan told me, "You know, I'm going to close escrow in two more weeks, and guess what? As I predicted, the stock is worth $350,000."

I said, "Well, you need to sell it."

No surprise to me, he commented, "No. There's going to be a big announcement coming out in a few days, and I think it's going to go to $400,000."

Well, the big announcement came out, and the announcement was that there was some sort of delay or issue with their software. The stock value plunged. It was now worth $150,000, which was going to leave him short on how much cash he needed for the down payment. The close of escrow came and, being short $100,000, he had to cancel escrow.

Shortly after that, 9/11 hit. The stock plunged and basically went to zero. Dan lost his opportunity. He'd had the ability to sell a stock that he bought for virtually nothing, earn enough money to buy an apartment building at an amazing time in the real estate market, and turn an amazing profit. Instead, he was too greedy, and he lost out entirely.

WHAT HAVE YOU TO LOSE?

"I bought my first property when I was nineteen. It was a duplex in Capistrano Beach. I was able to put together the $24,000 down payment by buying, fixing, and reselling old cars. That line of work started when I was fourteen. I bought a Mustang for $500, fixed it, and sold it for $1,200, and that inspired me to start flipping vehicles, which eventually led to my first foray into real estate. Still, it would be many years before I made real estate my career."

—FRED LEEDS

Here's something I hear from many new clients. "I want to buy a massive amount of buildings, but I don't know where I will be able to obtain the funds to make those purchases. I don't know how and when I will have that much money available."

You have a few options: Finding the cash from either investors or your own resources that you can tap into; or increasing the value of the properties that you purchase so that when you sell it or refinance it, it's worth more money.

EQUITY

Real estate brokers or mortgage brokers would be thrilled to help you determine how much equity you have available in the properties that you already own. They would be happy to take a look at everything under your umbrella:

your house, your duplex, your stock portfolio, the office building, that apartment building, in order to figure out if there is equity that can be pulled out.

If there is equity, then your next step is to determine the cost to pull that equity out. Refinancing a loan costs money. You have to pay the mortgage broker, appraiser, title, and escrow. Sometimes, you have a prepayment penalty to pay off your existing loan. There's an expense involved with this, so you have to make sure that it's worth the cost.

However, pulling out equity provides you with instant funding for your next purchase. If you've already followed your plan and identified a heavily-devalued property, you've positioned yourself to create wealth in a new building. The short-term costs you've incurred are far outweighed by future gains.

RAISING RENT

If you want to simply increase the value of the property that you already own, there are a number of ways to do it. The fastest, as we've discussed earlier, is to simply raise rents. Think of a twenty-unit apartment building where eight of the rents are $300 below market. You could probably increase the rents in those units by $150 a month and the tenants wouldn't go anywhere because moving is never easy and they're still receiving a relatively attractive deal, depending of course on the condition of their unit and their financial ability to pay more in rent. If an apartment's worth $1,200 and a tenant is paying $900 and you raise it to $1,050, the tenant is likely going to be staying rather than moving.

It should be said that raising rent isn't always a simple process. If the tenants are protected from even modest increases through rent control laws such as in New York City, San Francisco, or Los Angeles, there are maximums imposed based on your jurisdiction. If it's in Los Angeles, maybe you can raise it 3 percent annually and the majority of the state of California and Oregon is 7 percent to 10 percent. If you live in Arizona, or Pennsylvania, or Texas, you can probably do whatever you like.

The bottom line is this: If you're able to raise the rents and keep your tenants, you have effectively increased the value of the property without spending a cent. If it's a major difference between the current rent and market value, you can expect to see a substantial increase in your potential loan against the property. That one rent increase could be an additional 10 percent of a loan that the lender will provide to you, which would drastically move the needle on your ability to pull money out of the property.

1031 EXCHANGES

If you still don't have enough money to make a meaningful

new purchase to add to your growing portfolio, you can sell one of your buildings and enter into a "1031 tax deferred exchange." A 1031 is the IRS tax code involving what they call a Starker-Like Kind Exchange. This is a tax-deferred real estate transaction. If you meet all of the requirements under the IRS tax code 1031, you effectively can sell a property, buy another property, and defer your capital gains tax for the eventual sale of the new property.

If you buy a property for a million dollars and you sell it for $1.5 million, the IRS would say you have $500,000 of capital gain. On top of that, the IRS makes you depreciate the property annually. You might have an additional $100,000 of depreciation. Instead of the IRS saying you have $500,000 of capital gain, they'd also say you have $100,000 of depreciation recapture for a total of $600,000 in capital gain, which you would have to pay taxes on.

But if you execute a 1031, they will basically say that the $600,000 gain is deferred.

Let's just say you now buy a building for $2 million, and five years later you sell this building for $3 million. You would have a million dollar capital gain plus maybe $100,000 of depreciation recapture for $1.1 million. If you sold the property you would owe the IRS capital gains of $1.1 million for that transaction plus $600,000 for the first property. You'd have $1.7 million of capital gains taxes to pay on that.

Of course, these numbers are all approximate and your accountant would figure out all of the details.

The trick is to keep doing these exchanges so you don't ever have to pay taxes, at least in your lifetime. That is how people quickly grow their real estate portfolios. They either: 1) buy with their own money if they have a great source of income; 2) buy with investor's money if they have that at their disposal; 3) buy buildings, reposition them by raising rents, improving the value, refinance or sell them and use the sale or refinance proceeds to buy their next building.

You could simply find an investor—friends, family, colleagues, somebody who has money who wants to invest—and go that route. Rao Yamanchili says, "The second property I bought, a friend that was working at Xerox split the down payment with me. While on a doctor's visit, I mentioned that I was buying apartments. By the third property I bought, my doctor put up some money and the friend from Xerox came in with two other people, so now I had a total of four investors.

DEFINING YOUR GOALS

"Early on, I was fooled into buying properties just because they were cheap. We were buying mostly small properties and they were a lot of work."

—KEITH WASSERMAN

Determining what route to take when assessing your financial situation requires you to be very honest about your goals. In Chapter 1, I said you need to have a plan when you are acquiring properties. That plan should be to move you closer to your goals. But how do you define your goals, both short and long term?

When I sit down with a potential client, that's one of my first questions: "What are your long-term goals?" If their long-term goal is they want to go from owning two apartment buildings to owning twenty, that's a great long-term goal to have because it's obtainable and we can easily create a path forward using short-term milestones. They're not planning on going from two to twenty buildings overnight.

So their short-term goal is, "How are we going to accomplish this?" The first thing they need is to look at their economic situation. Is there cash in the bank? Do they have equity in their buildings that they can tap into through refinances as we just discussed? Can they quickly perform some renovations and try to raise some rents before they refinance to increase loan amounts? Should they sell a building?

If they bought a building and it's not something they want to keep (because it's too small, too difficult to manage, too far away, or they've pushed it as hard as they can), what are their options? They've squeezed every last drop out of that lemon. They probably should sell that property.

Or if they have an investor in that building that they no longer want to own properties with, then they probably need to sell that building as well. They need to figure out where they're going to come up with the equity to move forward. Then they make their move.

They sell or they refinance a building and they come out with equity to work with. Then they have to start searching for buildings to move the liquidity into. That is arguably the number one problem investors have: Finding opportunities—as in finding buildings to purchase that fit their criteria. That is what I'd consider to be the number one opportunity that people have once they are already in the business.

That's why it is so important to consider your goals in this business. If you want to own a vast portfolio of commercial real estate, you need to constantly be on the lookout for your next deal to purchase. When you're in the middle of buying an apartment building, you're searching for the next one. When you're adding value and repositioning, you're still searching. When you're taking a break for lunch, you're continuing to search. Finding the next property is a short-term goal that never goes away. You're only as good as your next deal.

The billion dollar portfolio isn't built overnight. It comes from step after step, goal after goal, and purchase after purchase. Your very first milestone has to be raising the money for the *next* purchase. If that sounds like a difficult task, you're not alone.

When people are first getting started, their number one problem is coming up with the money to buy their first building. Then the number two problem—which never seems to go away—is finding properties to purchase that meet their criteria.

STOP CHECKING YOUR REARVIEW MIRROR

"We've all made mistakes. The worst thing you can do is leave money in the bank. It's not doing anything for you there. Otherwise, my biggest mistake is selling too soon. A few times I've regretted selling properties that later appreciated drastically."
—PAUL LING

A common issue is that people are, in general, afraid of change. People are risk-averse, and the truth is that most weren't always that way. There was a point in everyone's life where they were less risk averse. They were more willing to take a gamble. They were just getting started. They felt time was on their side and they were willing to make investments that maybe were a little bit riskier, but because of where they were in their life, they were willing to do it.

Then later on they became risk averse. They're less willing

to refinance a property and put the largest possible loan on the building. They're less willing to sell a property and go into an exchange and then feel forced to buy something else. They're less willing to go buy a property that's not in an "A" location. They're risk-averse and that becomes a major problem for people who want to expand and grow their business.

It's an old expression, but true: most people keep looking in the rearview mirror. Remembering how easy things were back in the day and making excuses about why they can't replicate the same investment today.

Just like earlier, when we spoke about managing your greed, you also need to manage your fear and your expectations. That type of property you are looking at right now might be priced slightly higher than when you first started looking six months ago. You can't keep looking back, hoping to somehow *will* those previous prices back into existence. If you focus on what properties previously were worth, you're never going to make a deal happen. In a few months, that building will be worth a little more. Or maybe it will drop, but you'll have lost some money on another venture and won't have the capital to make the purchase.

Some other old expressions: "When I was a kid, gas was twenty-five cents a gallon." "When I was a kid we had to walk for five miles, through snow two feet deep to get to school."

No one cares about where prices were ten years ago, or even one year ago. As a broker, one of the most annoying questions people ask me when we are marketing a property for sale is, "What did the current owner pay for the property ten years ago?" It would be rude for me to tell them the truth, which is that it's irrelevant.

You buy buildings today because you think you can make them work tomorrow, either for immediate cash flow, or you think it has great long-term potential. You don't sit there and complain about what the property would have been worth way back when, because basically you're just looking back in time, and that's not taking you anywhere. The most successful people that I ever dealt with could care less what a property was worth in the past. Rao Yalamanchili even told me that they have bought buildings that they previously owned and sold a decade ago. Savvy investors will look at a property and think, "What can I buy it for today? What can I do to increase the value? What will this deal be worth in two, three years?"

A property might sell at some point for say $1 million. The second time for $1.5 million. The third time for $2.5 million. The fourth time the property is worth $5 million. If the guy that bought it for $3.5 million was to say, "This building was worth $2.5 million a year ago," he would never have bought it, and would have never gotten to take advantage of it appreciating all the way to $5 million.

It's no different than the people who buy stocks and say, "Well, Microsoft was $5. Then it went to $20. Then it went to $200. I don't want to buy at $200 because it might drop to $5 again. I don't think it can go from $200 to $300, or even $220." Those are the people that shouldn't be doing any form of investing. They should just keep money in the bank, or buy United States treasuries, because they're afraid of an economic collapse that may or may not ever happen.

When we talk about defining your goals, you need to stop and think: Who's driving your car? Professional race car drivers out on the track always look at where they want to get their car to. When they're entering into a turn, they're not looking directly in front of their car. They're looking in the direction of where they want to steer their car. They're making the assumption that what's right in front of them is going to be okay, so they focus their eyesight by turning their head towards where they want their car to be after they come out of the turn. If they don't get back on the gas at the earliest opportunity, they lose momentum.

If you lose momentum in this business, you're out of the race.

When you're buying commercial real estate, my advice is to

not be looking at what the property was worth two years ago let alone what it sold for twenty years ago. That is ancient history. You're looking at where you can take the building to in the future. You're looking down the road and saying, "If I renovate this, I can move these rents to here and I can then sell or refinance." The people that become insanely wealthy in this business are the people that have the vision and confidence to take this risk.

I've had clients that went through periods where they didn't buy any buildings. "Things are too expensive," they say. Then suddenly, out of nowhere, they buy twenty buildings.

"Wow, how'd that happen?" I ask.

They all have different reasons such as, "Well, my son wanted to get into the business." Or, "Someone I was talking to made me realize that I've been a big baby and I haven't been taking chances."

Whatever the impetus, they remembered, "Hey, I want to keep buying buildings."

TIMING THE MARKET

"During the Great Recession of 2007 and 2008, I learned LAX [Los Angeles International Airport] was expanding and needed to buy apartment buildings in the airport's proposed flight path

[where I owned a few]. Three things worked in my favor: I had converted the apartments to condominiums, which made them worth more, and the airport was offering above-market prices. As a result, I was able to cash out at a time when real estate prices were low. This gave me more money to buy other properties at a time in the market when prices were low and more attractive for buying."

—PAUL LING

There is no such thing as a stable market. It's like the tide; it's always going up or down. Buying at the bottom is great, because you know that the building you want to purchase was worth considerably more in a prior market. You're buying the building with the aspirations that if you hold it long enough, once you come out of the recession, the value of the property should go back up and you've made money just through holding power.

You've probably heard the expression, "Buy Low, Sell High." It's just as simple as that. Andrew Tavakoli says, "80 percent of wealth is created simply through appreciation of timing," which means that most investors can truly state that timing is everything. Buying while the market is rising has created the majority of the wealth that most real estate owners have.

As I've said previously, there is no "bottom" to a market for timing purchases, so you might find yourself chasing rising prices. Buying on the way up lets you take advantage of the trend. You see that the rents are rising, you see the values are rising, and you jump on the bandwagon. That's also an easy no-brainer investment.

But when you're at the top of the market, you don't always *know* you're at the top of the market. There's no light flashing on Wall Street that says, "Top of the market." You never know, just like you never know you're at the bottom. That's where a little due diligence can save you from a substantial investment in a property with nowhere to grow.

It's important to remember that we aren't buying stocks. Some people tell their stockbroker, "I want to buy a hundred shares of a stock in brand X. It's currently selling at $20 a share and when it gets down to $15, just buy me as much of it as you can." This business of purchasing commercial real estate doesn't work like that. You might not ever buy, because prices might not ever drop to the level that you desire. But if you wait, you will have missed out on the cash flow and appreciation that you would otherwise have achieved by jumping in.

If you're nervous about the market, don't take on a large new investment. Don't spend all your available cash on one large transaction. If you think the market might drop and you have a million dollars, don't spend all of it on one building. Maybe use $300,000 and buy a smaller building. Make a meaningful investment, but save a little money for the next deal or for a rainy day.

PLAYING WELL WITH OTHERS

"I had between ten and twelve partners at one point, but most have retired and now I have none. Now, my kids are involved in the business."

—RAO YALAMANCHILI

If you've explored every option and you still aren't sure where to find money for your next purchase, you can always explore becoming involved with investors.

Syndicating properties is simply purchasing properties with investor's money. These investors are each contributing funds and each is expecting some sort of return in exchange. There's obviously positives and negatives to entering into business in this manner.

The positives always appear to be straight forward: You're using your investors' money to buy a deal you otherwise couldn't afford, and you can significantly scale your business. The negative is that all the pressure for success rides on you. If the property performs well, you look like a hero. If it doesn't, you look like a goat and there is a good possibility that your investors (and their attorneys) will entirely blame you as the person who screwed it up.

Your investors probably want some sort of meaningful return. If the building doesn't perform well, you're going to be responsible for paying them back whatever you promised them as the minimum annual return. If you don't have the means to pay them, you have to probably sell the property at a loss or cut them checks from your personal funds.

It's a different type of an investment, and I don't recommend it for those just starting out.

YOU HAVE TO SPEND MONEY TO MAKE MONEY

"I was born in Iran and came to the U.S. with an engineering degree that I earned in England. I planned to get my master's degree here, but when the Shah was deposed in the 1970s, my parents could no longer support my studies. I got into the export/import business for a while before borrowing money from family members to purchase an office building with a friend. I have since refinanced that property three or four times. That's what I call the dream of real estate—to buy, increase value, and pull out all of your initial investment."

—DAVID POURBABA

Buying commercial properties is a very expensive investment, but one with a very lucrative potential return. Even if you have a few buildings in your portfolio, I find it best to start small and work your way up. From what I've learned with my clients and my own experience, that is a far more feasible path to success.

Say someone owns a house. To expand, they buy another

house with the intentions of making it a rental. Then they buy a duplex, then a four-unit building, then an eight-unit building. The next thing they know, they refinance some money out of the buildings and they go out and buy a twenty-unit apartment building. It's just the natural path that most people take when they're spending their own money. They slowly and steadily work their way up.

It's like going to the gym. You start out on one particular exercise with twenty pounds of weight, and then a year later you're pushing thirty pounds of weight around and the following year forty. You have to slowly grow stronger, and it takes some time.

As you're settling into this business, don't sweat it if you're starting out slow. As long as you're building momentum and taking calculated risks, you're moving forward. Just remember that building a billion dollar portfolio means *always* being on the lookout for the next property to purchase. Most importantly, it means *buying* that next property.

Don't think you have the cash needed? You probably have equity in the property you already own. You could call a bank and receive a loan so that you can buy a larger property and start building from there. If you're worried about becoming overleveraged, don't spend everything you have available on one enormous building. As David Pourbaba says, buying real estate is, "Like taking a kid to a candy store, you need to be careful. Don't get carried away and buy the wrong deal at the wrong price and terms."

If you want that billion dollar portfolio, you need to keep buying. Danny Monempour grew his portfolio by setting realistic goals and then exceeding them. His goal was to purchase 100 units per year, and he's consistently exceeded that. He took on investors as he could further scale his business that way. "I can do ten deals (with investors) or only three (with my own money)."

Once you have the properties, then it's time to start thinking about renovations.

CHAPTER 3

———

MAKING MONEY WITH RENOVATIONS

"The first thing we do is take care of any deferred maintenance. We can't control those costs and it's easier to get them over with in the beginning. You always get hurt when you sell a building with an infrastructure problem like a bad roof or bad plumbing. After that work is done, we reposition all our buildings with light renovations. We do kitchens, bathrooms, aesthetics. We want clean, aesthetically pleasing and safe workforce housing on a budget."

—BOB HART

I bought an apartment building in 2014 and decided I was going to renovate it. Not just a few things; I wanted to make this property look like a new building. I took whatever money I had left over after the purchases and started looking for good places to spend it. I didn't stop to think about where I could find the best return on investment. It was like the money was burning a hole in my pocket and I had to get rid of it.

I redid the landscaping, the roof, and added all sorts of aesthetic improvements. Then, when I tried to reposition the tenants to add value, I hit a major stumbling block.

What I failed to consider: tenants of properties—whether apartments, retail or office—care about two things: One, is their rent affordable to them? Two, is their rent a decent value for them? When you paint the outside of the building, that doesn't really help the tenant out at all. The tenants are already there. They don't care that you just made the building look prettier on the outside. They're already in their space. They're never staring at the exterior of the building. Maybe it looks better when their friends, family, and someone that they want to impress comes over, but they're not going to be willing to pay more rent now. Maybe retail and office tenants care more as it affects their customers and retail traffic, but if they don't shortly see an immediate improvement, they certainly aren't going to want to pay for upgrades that were made that did nothing to help their business. And if they're thinking about moving regardless, they're not all of a sudden going to say, "You know what? I'm not going to leave because the landlord just painted the outside of the building." That's not going to change anything.

I made a rookie mistake, and it's one I've seen dozens of times since.

Renovations are meant to improve the value of the building. Aesthetics are great, but they age quickly. Landscaping can make a property more attractive, but it's almost always costly to maintain. When you start making choices meant to add value to your property, it helps to have a long-term plan in mind. So where do you start?

PAINTING THE ROSES RED

"Two of the most important long-term renovations are plumbing and roof. In the long run, provided the building is a long-term hold, it's much better and cheaper to eliminate deferred maintenance."

—ABE STEIN

If you're about to sell the building, or if you have three units that are becoming vacant and the building just looks absolutely terrible, you're not going to accomplish your pricing goal when the outside of the building looks horrible. You're going to have to reasonably improve its appearance if you expect to hit retail plus pricing. Rao Yamanchili usually focuses on exterior improvements rather than major renovations. "I avoid structural work and focus on cosmetics. The best renovations are exterior improvements that increase the value of the property."

The question becomes how much can you allocate towards each repair. More specifically, it comes down to how effectively you can increase the rent. Owners need to create their own internal formula of how much they're willing to spend on an improvement versus how much higher the rent can be increased after that improvement is implemented.

For instance, an apartment that was previously rented at around $1,000 becomes vacant. The unit is in very rough condition and it needs to be renovated. If you invest $5,000 into renovations to the apartment, maybe you can increase the rent to $1,200 a month. That means you'd receive a $200 monthly increase, which is $2,400 a year. Over two years, you've netted an additional $4,800 total. You almost earn your entire investment back in two years. That's almost a 50 percent annual return on your investment! Good luck finding that in the stock market.

But if you spent $20,000 on the unit, and then you raise the rent from $1,000 to $1,400, you've only increased the rent by almost $5,000 a year. It's then going to take you four years to recoup your investment. That is still a good business plan if you are planning on selling or refinancing the property, but for maximum cash flow and minimizing your expenses, it's not.

With the $5,000 upgrade, which would maybe just be paint, flooring, and some other light renovations, you should get all your money back in two years. For the same price as the fancier renovation, you can cover four times the number of units.

Another common choice for a capital improvement is a new roof. We mentioned this earlier, but if you're looking at a heavily devalued building and the roof needs replacing, you should include that in the purchase price. A new roof is not a small amount of money. If you've already purchased the property and now you're shelling out $50,000 for a new roof, you're burning money that could be better spent elsewhere to actually net you additional cash flow.

On another point, and I'm no accountant, spending money on repairs has the upside of typically being a one-year write-off for your taxes, but check with your accountant as sometimes what you think is a repair, such as replacing all of the windows or the roof, the IRS considers a capital improvement that needs to be depreciated over a period of around ten to 30 years, which means you only get a small annual write-off and you can't take it all at once to offset capital gains.

So instead of replacing the entire roof, you can send a roofer up once a year for $1,000 and have the contractor patch and maintain the roof to keep it in serviceable condition. You can drastically extend the life of a roof this way, but eventually you or the next owner will need to replace it. You can only kick that can down the road for so long.

Adding a $50,000 roof to a property is not going to increase the rents or the overall value of the property anywhere near the amount that you just spent on it. You're not going to be able to convince the tenants to pay more in rent because you put on a new roof. The tenants don't care. They expect there to be a decent roof.

However, if the roof is so destroyed that there's constant leaks and tenants are getting flooded apartments and water damage, then you probably will be able to charge a higher rent by replacing the roof because you've probably been discounting the rent to account for this mess. Not to mention legal issues with your tenants resulting from ongoing leaks and the costs of repairs resulting from roof leaks. Your current tenants probably aren't willing to pay as much money because there are problems with the building. If you are able to make an extra one or two thousand per month by investing in a $50,000 roof, it will pay itself off as a medium- to long-term investment.

You'll see the same returns with plumbing. If there's no water pressure or inconsistent water in the building, the tenants aren't going to pay as much rent, so you might want to fix that problem. However, you don't want to go spend $100,000 re-piping a building just because the plumbing is aging and needs an occasional repair. You're not going to be able to quickly recoup that investment on the building.

To summarize: Your goal is to try and make meaningful capital improvements that result in you being able to increase the rents enough to recoup your investment in a time period that you feel is acceptable.

TIME FOR AN UPGRADE

"For apartment buildings, paint and landscaping are the best ways to boost the value when selling. Those improvements are inexpensive. For retail properties, we recoat and restripe the parking lot and take care of any visible problem resulting from deferred maintenance. If someone can walk or drive past a building and see signs of deferred maintenance, we will need to take care of it before selling."

—RAND SPERRY

The time to make cosmetic improvements to the exterior of the property—or the common areas, the walkways, the hallways—is when you have units that are going to be coming up for rent. It's not worth spending another $50,000 just to get fifty bucks a month in rent from one unit.

You have to be very cognizant of where you're spending your money. You could spend $100,000 cleaning up a building and making it look attractive, and then all of a sudden the building next door comes up for sale and you don't have enough money to buy it because you just wasted your precious funds painting your property for no good business reason.

David Soufer prefers to spend drastically less on renovations and achieve a slightly lower rent as opposed to gut-renovating a unit and charging a slightly higher rent. His business plan involves much less capital contributions for unit renovations but results in much better long-term cash flow. This makes excellent short- and long-term sense.

Spend your money on items that are going to help you make additional money. You don't replace a roof just because it's ten years old. You replace a roof when you absolutely have to, when patching isn't going to properly repair it.

You don't replace *all* the windows just because one is broken. You don't redo the entire plumbing system just because you have one pinhole leak in the building. You have to spend your money wisely, and you have to spend it in a way that maximizes the income of the property.

Now, if the windows and plumbing are completely beyond their useful life and you're preparing to replace them, it might be worth the added expense to just renovate the entire building. Since you're already buying a large quantity of windows, you might be able to negotiate a deal that saves you money in the long run by creating a larger economy of scale. You'll have to take a look at your formula to see how much of an increase is needed to recoup the costs, or how this expense will affect your valuation.

Note that renovations are not the same as ongoing maintenance. For all of the aesthetics and appliances you'll own in a property, a little money up front can and will save you thousands of dollars in the long run. Be smart with your finances.

Sometimes, you're going to have to spend substantial money for a larger repair. Let's say you have a few plumbing leaks reported. You call a few plumbers to solicit bids (always try to obtain several bids) and three of the plumbers return to you with estimates for the job. They all offer to perform the work for around $3,000, but one of the plumbers goes further. He says, "Well, I could do the repair, but I'm probably going to be back here in six months because there's some other repairs that need to be made. I could do the whole thing now for five grand." If you take the quick fix, it's going to cost you a thousand bucks every year for the foreseeable future. Maybe it's best to spend the additional money and be done with it.

You have to ask yourself, "Am I better off in the long term

making this massive repair now or doing a half-measure repair that kicks the can down the road on the real problem?" This is why so many buildings that are eighty years old have eighty-year-old electrical and plumbing in them; because the owner could never justify the expense of making the upgrade.

If you decide to invest in a major upgrade, be aware of new building codes. For instance, in the 1990s, you could install a whole new electrical system for a forty-unit apartment building for $10,000. In 2020, that would be a $150,000 job because the codes have changed. There now needs to be four times the number of outlets and circuits in every unit. You have to space outlets two feet apart from each other in the kitchen. The costs to do improvements on electrical and plumbing tends to go higher as cities change their building codes.

There's a reason for all these new codes. We've learned about overloading circuits and preventing fires. A number of these fixes are for the health and welfare of the tenant. That doesn't mean it makes that added cost any easier to swallow, but maybe it softens the blow. My advice? Don't buy buildings that have electrical issues, and if the plumbing is an issue, gain a good understanding of what it's going to take to fix the situation before you buy it.

Finally, remember that any renovation takes an investment

of time as well as capital. Jerry Fink warns not to make a common mistake. "I was trying to do too much myself instead of hiring vendors. What would have taken two months took four."

AESTHETIC CHOICES THAT MAKE SENSE

"I renovate properties with the idea that I wouldn't be ashamed to have one of my relatives living there. I take great pride in creating and helping communities, and it's important to me to have tenants love living at one of my properties."

—THOMAS SAFRAN

There are two areas to improve a property: mechanical and cosmetic. We just talked about mechanical: the pipes, the wiring and the roof. Let's take a closer look at the question of cosmetic upgrades.

Michael Sorochinsky focuses on what he calls the Leasing Path. "A prospective tenant sees the outside of the property, the lobby, the landscaping; everything must look right, feel right, and smell right. They see the cosmetics. If you can't increase rents, then there is no business plan. The biggest bang for the buck is cosmetics."

Cosmetic fixes have their time and place. I don't want you leaving this book thinking there is no point to landscaping or painting. If your tenants think they live in a run-down building, it doesn't matter that you installed new sinks. It's the same with the classic car. If you spend all your time and money on new leather seats and a rebuilt motor, but the outside is just rusted and dented metal, you're not going to sell it, or at least get a reasonable price for it. Sometimes, you have to spend the money to make the property cosmetically attractive.

You resurface the driveway, or touch up the landscaping, or repaint the hallways, and add new fixtures to the common area. Those are cosmetic improvements.

Mechanical items are very important. If the building has faulty wiring or lousy pipes, your tenants will complain and leave, unless of course the rent is so low that they will suffer through it, which isn't your goal. However, those are the things that the tenants don't pay you a dollar extra for. The tenants just assume when they move into a building that the plumbing, the electrical, and the roof are in good working order. When you go through the building and you make massive upgrades, oftentimes the tenants don't even notice. They don't know that you just replaced most of the plumbing. How would they?

If you're going to make cosmetic upgrades, you need to think long and hard about how to spend your money wisely. I see many people make mistakes in this area. They will paint a part of the property that nobody can see, like the back of the building. The only one who ever goes back there is the guy from the utility company to read the electric meters. I'm sure he could care less about the new designer color.

Maybe they install a fancy sink in the laundry room, or put new flooring in the boiler room. What I tell people is, "Don't treat your building like your home." If you're a homeowner, you want everything to be perfect. You want to upgrade every closet and windowpane, because it's your home. It's understandable.

A rental property, however, is an investment. So only spend money on the things that matter, where you can achieve the best return on investment. This means improvements that let you increase rent and retain great tenants. Don't paint your boiler room. Spend your money making the front of the building look great, make the lobby attractive, and make vacant units look amazing.

REPOSITIONING TENANTS AND UNITS

"From a money-making standpoint, it doesn't make sense to extensively renovate units that are already producing good rent. It's not worth spending $20,000 on improvements to get $200 more a month in rent. It's better to spend less and not increase the rent as much."

—DAVID POURBABA

Don't go in and renovate a tenant's unit unless you can immediately afterwards reposition the lease rate in your favor.

I have to tell clients this all the time. If you already have someone living in a unit, and they're content, don't go in and start making major improvements. That's a big challenge for people. Newer property owners feel compelled to go renovate a tenant's unit every few years.

I ask them, "Is the tenant paying market? Are they going to pay a higher rent if you go in and you make those repairs?" I tell them it's like owning a used car. When you buy a brand new car, you expect everything to be great: engine, transmission, upholstery, navigation system, stereo. When the car is ten years old, do you expect the paint to be perfect? No. The engine or transmission to be perfect? No. For the car to look great, smell great on the inside? No. It's a decade old.

If a tenant's been living in a unit for ten years, that tenant can't expect to have the same quality of apartment as someone who just moved into the unit next door paying $500 more per month. They're probably paying well below market since they've been living there so long, which they'll understand comes with a few caveats. If that tenant wants their apartments to be beautiful and shiny, then offer to move them into the next vacant unit in exchange for them paying market value.

In life, you get what you pay for. This tends to be a very challenging thing to explain to property owners (as well as tenants) because they don't want trouble with their tenants. Remember that these are your customers, and you want them to be happy, but that doesn't mean you have to move mountains. You are a property owner, a business person.

Eventually, you'll have tenants who move out for one reason or another. Once that happens, you want to move as quickly and efficiently as possible. Every day that an apartment or commercial space sits idle is a day you're burning through money. You should start planning your renovations before they actually move out. However, as I just mentioned that David Pourbaba told me, "Don't spend too much money on upgrades when you have a vacancy if you are already getting good rent on the unit." What he means is that if the vacant unit is already in good enough condition to rent for close to what a gut-renovated unit would achieve, then leave it the way it is!

If an apartment or commercial space is worth $2,000 a month, every day that it's vacant is going to cost roughly $70 per day. That's a challenge. You must figure out what to do. If it's going to take you two months to undergo a gut renovation, can you absorb that cost? A lighter renovation might only take two weeks. Paint and flooring can take you days.

You have to figure out how much work a unit needs to charge to the rent levels that you're projecting. That's where you have to perform an analysis, otherwise called a market rent survey. You, or your property manager, will need to look at comparable units that are for rent and compare them to your vacancies.

If you have a solid property manager (which we will talk about later), they should provide you with several options for your next vacancy, such as this:

Dear Property Owner,

We've inspected the unit that became vacant and we feel there are three renovation options:

The first option is a simple cleanup for $5,000. We can clean the unit, paint the walls, and rip out the carpet and replace it with laminate flooring. That will take one week, and the new rent will be around $1,000 per month.

Option two is a partial remodel. We can install a new countertop, new appliances in the kitchen, renovate the bathroom with a new toilet, new vanity, new mirror. Then we will tile the bathroom and kitchen floors. The rest of the unit will get real hardwood throughout. That's going to cost $10,000 and take three weeks, and the new rent will be around $1,200 per month.

Option three is a complete gut remodel of the apartment. We *will put in a new kitchen and bathroom, add recessed lighting, new windows, new tile or wood flooring everywhere. That will cost $20,000 and take six weeks. Your new rent will be closer to $1,400 per month.*

You then have to decide which option makes the most sense. The first thing you have to ask is how much money you have available and are there other improvements you absolutely need to perform. Some owners have a maintenance schedule and need money for upcoming projects. Some owners have period capital distributions to investors and need to reserve cash for that purpose. Do you have to replace the roof anytime soon? Are there any other major capital improvements coming up that you can't avoid?

Second of all, is it worth doing the job? Is it worth spending an extra $10,000 just to earn an extra $200 a month more on rent? The answer is probably not. That extra $200 in rent is $2,400 a year. That means you won't recoup the cost for another four years at least. But still that's an additional 25 percent annualized return, way better than you are going to find elsewhere. But remember that tenants who are paying top-of-the market lease rates tend to move out faster than more below market rents, and the units take longer to rent at premium levels.

Not to mention it's going to take you an extra month of vacancy to complete the renovations, which means you're giving up $1,000 in rent to complete the job. The renovation is now costing you an extra $11,000 ($10,000 of extra work and $1,000 of lost rent). Add to that the extra aggravation of having to deal with all those contractors and have construction in the building, which will annoy all the other tenants for an additional period of time and potentially bring the city in to start asking for permits and look for other issues to complain about.

It's best to perform an analysis on your return on investment. If your plan is to sell the building or to refinance it very quickly, it's probably worth it to go all out on the larger renovation. Another $2,400 per year of rent could make the building worth another $25,000 in valuation. If the lender is going to give you a 60 percent LTV (loan to value) refinance loan on the property, that's another $15,000 in refinance proceeds you'll pull out after the refinance is closed, which makes this upfront cost easier to justify.

If you go to sell the building, it's the same thing. The new buyer is going to pay you an additional $25,000 for the building, and it only cost you $10,000. It's a $15,000 profit. For those reasons, I typically think it's worth spending the extra time and money.

THE PROOF IS IN THE PURCHASE

"Ninety percent of the time, we put from $3,000 to $10,000

into each unit. We don't over-improve the unit for the area it's in, but we do add value. We like to run our buildings like a Honda—we're practical and efficient."

—KEITH WASSERMAN

Raising rent isn't just about cash flow. It's to demonstrate to future buyers, your investors, and lenders that the building is a viable investment. That it will keep pace with the market and be a worthy long-term asset. That's why renovations are such an important part of this business. You need to perform a cost analysis to figure out how you can reposition the building by doing that work.

Remember, if you can take a $1,000 per rent unit and make it worth $1,400, you can then make a strong argument to a prospective buyer and lender that every unit in the building is worth $1,400 a month or maybe even more. Therefore, you have proven that the building has so much more long-term upside potential. This is one of the number one reasons to spend that money, to prove the potential rent of the property, to prove the rental upside.

Proven upside is a really important thing. I can't tell you how often we see buildings that are for sale and the broker or owners are telling us, "Oh, these one bedrooms are worth $1,500 per month." Then we look at the rent roll and we see that the owner just rented two of the one-bedroom units at $1,200.

A natural reaction would be, "Hold on. How is *that* apartment worth $1,500 when the owner hasn't been able to achieve more than $1,200?"

The owner never has a believable explanation. "Well, I just didn't want to spend any money on that unit." Why not? If you knew you were going to be selling, why wouldn't you spend a little bit more money so that you could charge a higher rent and validate your claim? Now, unless you own a building nearby and really feel that you can reach $1,500, you might not have much confidence that you can actually *achieve* those rents. The savvy owner knows that he needs to prove it to buyers. He's going to go ahead and make those improvements and push the rent to prove to buyers that these units really are worth $1,500 and that the other units at $1,200 have proven upside.

That's the difference between the average property owner and the really successful one. This is where you start moving toward the billion-dollar portfolio. The people that make the most money are willing to spend the extra time and capital to reposition vacant units per their business plan, which includes their short- and long-term goals.

However, that method only works if you're looking to refinance or sell relatively soon. All improvements wear out with age, both physically and cosmetically. Styles change. If you spent $20,000 and fully renovated a unit, but then you waited ten years to sell, all of those improvements are now outdated and worth much less, and it will show in your lease rates.

Some of you might fall into a third category. You never refinance and you rarely sell. This building is meant to be a constant cash flow generator. In that case, you'll probably go with the second option from a few pages back regarding unit renovations. You might spend $10,000 on the vacancy, but recoup that cost over a shorter time period. If you're keeping the building for ten or twenty years, it's going to quickly recover that cost.

The owner who buys buildings and quickly repositions and then sells them is doing everything that they can to achieve the highest possible rent when a unit becomes vacant. They need to maximize the rental rate to show a lender (for cash-out refinancing) or a buyer (for a profitable sale) that the entire building is worth that higher rent.

The owner who holds on to a building long term doesn't have to prove anything to anybody. They know that every year they are going to be giving all of their tenants a small but meaningful rent increase. After several years, they're going to have the unit at $1,400 and they will have spent less money on renovations, provided the tenant doesn't leave.

You have to make renovations that are smart, and—as we've

mentioned time and time again—you have to manage your greed. I worked with a client who went way overboard on renovations in the pursuit of the impossible.

This guy planned to sell his property, and his goal naturally was achieving the highest possible price he could fetch for it. After some renovations, he was able to charge $1,800 for a unit. That wasn't enough. He wanted to hit $2,000. So he spent more and more money, added all the bells and whistles you can imagine, and he finally started renting units at $2,000.

Then he went to sell the building. The buyer's lender obtained an appraisal for the purpose of a new loan. The lender said, "Our appraiser thinks that these units are worth $1,800. You managed to lease them for $2,000, which is great, but our appraiser thinks those units are above market. We're only going to give you credit for $1,800 and we are going to base our loan on that lease rate." Of course, the buyer figures the rents are above market and there is downside risk in the lease rates, making this seem like a risky investment. After all of his hard work and money, the seller ended up taking a hit because he over improved. It's similar to that expression: You don't want to be the most expensive house on the block. In this situation, you don't want to be the highest rent in the area.

I have a client with this exact problem right now. He owns

a thirty-unit building, which he gave me to sell, and all of his studio apartments are at $1,525 monthly. His neighbor, who owns a similar building across the street, wanted to buy his building, but the neighbor's property manager informed him: "I don't think these units are worth more than $1,400, maybe $1,450 maximum."

The neighbor was concerned. "You know, it's great that your seller has renovated twenty units, but we're not comfortable with the lease rates as we have concerns that they are not sustainable. We think all those units should be $1,400 and not $1,525. Therefore, we're not willing to pay you the price that your seller wants because we have issues with the lease rates."

My client checked around with comparable units, and he was certainly on the high end of the spectrum. If the market held out, eventually he'd be with the rest of the pack. Unfortunately, this buyer didn't have confidence that the market would head in that direction.

In that situation, you should look for another buyer or lender. Don't take the loss just yet. If you did your research and you're confident that the market is on your side, stick to your guns. You'll find a like-minded buyer eventually. That said, sometimes you overextend yourself and you'll need to be prepared to swallow some of that cost. That's the business.

HOW TO SELL A GOLDEN GOOSE

"I purchase buildings that are 'above water,' try to make them slightly better, then hold onto them. I avoid buying buildings that need complete renovations. Instead, I buy buildings that are in decent shape and then focus on improvements to the common areas, hallways, lobby, elevator areas, and kitchens and bathrooms. Then I set rents just below the market value to ensure tenants continue to pay rent."

—DAVID SOUFER

Renovations and repositioning are critical tools to get the most return on your real estate investment. While most buyers understand the basics of cosmetic or mechanical upgrades, it is important to do your research and have a solid plan before spending money to upgrade your property.

Remember that mechanical upgrades are very important to the life and longevity of your building but will likely not yield any short-term rent increases. Cosmetic upgrades are great for your valuation but only if done smartly and with a bit of forethought.

As for quality-of-life improvements, that all depends on your business plan. You might be able to coax your tenants to a higher rent, but you could also risk pushing too far past the market value of comparable buildings. Thomas Safran says, "I built properties to a level I'd be comfortable with relatives living there."

Most important of all, your renovations should be a part of your plan toward increasing the value of the units, enabling you to increase the lease rate. The more valuable the property, the more you can expect to receive from a lender on a refinance or a buyer on a sale.

As you build out your billion-dollar portfolio, you'll develop a better sense of how these pieces all fit into place. You'll also get a better instinct for which renovations are needed and which can be pushed off to a later date.

Once you've raised the expected value of your building, it's time to think about that crucial next step: Whether to refinance or sell on the way to your next purchase.

CHAPTER 4

REFINANCING OR SELLING

"Mortgage brokers are like drug dealers. Most drugs are misused and will kill you. Improperly used debt kills you, too. Always keep a 25 percent debt-to-equity ratio. That's how you survive recessions."

—FRED LEEDS

Picture a brand new car on a lot. It's shiny, fresh, and barely has ten miles on the odometer. This is the latest model, with every upgrade you can imagine. It's worth a fixed price, comparable to similar vehicles on the market. But once that new car is driven off the lot, it immediately loses major value.

The same thing happens to commercial real estate. Years after you've put in all the new, in-vogue designer cosmetic improvements, the value is going to drop. You have to know when to get out.

Years ago, I had a building that became something of a pet project. I loved it. The layout, structure, floor plans, and the facade. I hired an architect and invested tens of thousands of dollars on a massive cosmetic renovation to the exterior and units, making it a modern marvel that just called out to prospective tenants. The value shot right up. I had a great deal on my hands.

But I didn't sell it.

Month after month, year after year, I held onto that property and watched the price fluctuate. I wasn't really looking for a particular price, I just wasn't ready to sell. I had invested my time and money, and I wanted to reap the benefits for a little longer. As it turns out, I waited too long.

Buildings, like cars and hair styles, can eventually go out of fashion. Just like you don't see too many Hummers on the roads anymore, my style of renovations became dated. Tenants weren't as attracted to leasing the vacant units and paying premium rent anymore, and I couldn't achieve as high of a lease rate as I previously did in comparison with other properties, and the buyers knew they'd need a light cosmetic renovation to bring it up to the new "modern" aesthetic.

The lesson I learned, very much the hard way, is that you have to know when to sell.

WHY SELL SUCH A NICE PLACE?

"A big red flag is when the building's rents are higher than the going market rate. That's an unsustainable situation, and you're the one who pays the price for it. I prefer properties that have rents below the market rate. I'm also leery of properties that have vacant units."

—ABRAHAM STEIN

There are a few reasons people sell: They have to, they want to, or they're forced to. An old saying is that people sell because of death, divorce, or taxes. Some great reasons to sell properties are when they don't have much remaining rental upside, are having management problems, or you feel you can't raise the rents further.

There's another old saying, "You can't take it with you." When you are no longer with us, that building is going to belong to someone. If you've left it to a relative or spouse, that person may not want the responsibility that owning commercial real estate brings.

Some people sell because the expenses overtake them. They're overleveraged or spread too thin. Still others sell because they made a profit and are moving on to what they feel are greener pastures. Maybe they have investors who just want to take a profit and move on with their lives. Maybe they want to simply be rid of their investors. That happens all the time. Someone buys a building with several investors, and they cash out once they see a profit.

There are situations where people sell because they feel that they have maximized value on a property. They bought a building when the average rent was $1,000, and they moved it up to $1,400. They're managing their greed and are stepping out now that they've added as much value to the property as they feel they reasonably can.

Some people sell because they're paying attention to the market and they anticipate an economic correction coming. They want to get out before rents and values drop and they're left footing the bill, regretting not taking a profit.

Sometimes, people sell for the wrong reasons. Maybe the other investors don't want to put in additional money for necessary repairs or renovations. Maybe their partner wants to cash out and they can't find a new investor.

People sell for various reasons, but the idea we are going to focus on is people selling with the goal of making money. As Jeff Elowe says, "You can't go broke making a profit."

LEARNING FROM MY MISTAKES

"I should have been more aggressive and used my partners to buy more buildings. I should have added more partners and bought more buildings. I had the courage and conviction to buy and sell. I just knew when something was a good deal or not."

—ANDREW TAVAKOLI

As I mentioned at the beginning of this chapter, when a new car is driven off the lot, it instantaneously loses value as it's no longer considered "new," and the same thing happens to commercial buildings and apartments. Granted, you're very rarely going to be purchasing brand new construction. When you finish upgrading and renovating an office or apartment building, and after you've brought it up to modern cosmetic standards, the value is most likely going to start to slowly drop. The building has been fully renovated, it's as attractive as it's going to be, and it's usually time to move on. That's when you should consider selling, as it's the equivalent of a new car at the dealership.

I fell in love with a building—that I still own—on a street called Fountain (any Angelenos reading will be familiar). When I bought this building, it was very unattractive: it had wood siding, it was deteriorated, and it's what I would call a "dog." So I created a business plan with a budget, hired an architect who gave me what I thought was a beautiful design for a modern, hip cosmetic appearance, landscaping, and stucco design.

We re-stuccoed the building, and we gave it a really cool industrial look with earth-tone exterior colors because that's how new construction buildings looked at the time. After we finished the construction, I rented the units out for what I thought were top rents. I'd put so much time and energy into this project that I decided to turn it over to management and keep it long term for cash flow.

I had some offers that came in unsolicited, but I decided to refinance it instead. Looking back, the value of that building, adjusted over time, was well over what I collected. That said, I don't have any regrets. It was a lesson learned, and the building has still been a relatively headache-free cash generator.

Recently, an individual tenant began renting all the units from me, essentially running it as an Airbnb hotel. Instead of me charging $1,800 rent a month per each unit, she's paying me a premium at $2,000 for each unit a month. Then she's turning around and renting all the units out for $125 to $150 a night. She's profiting about $500 on each unit. It's a nice little cottage industry for herself.

The way I justified this was having one tenant paying all the bills. I receive one monthly check and I don't have to deal with any headaches, and the units are paying above market. It was as close to a triple-net investment as I could expect with the asset class, and it was a win-win for everybody, and it's all because I kept that building. Until, of course, she quit paying rent. April 2020 hit, the world shut down for the COVID-19 outbreak, and she had no nightly guests to rent to. Overnight, she couldn't pay the rent, and now I had a building with absolutely no income and the same expenses it always had. Big problem.

I could have sold it after an eighteen-month hold and made an enormous profit and moved on to the next deal, but I went a different route. My plan at the time wasn't to build a billion dollar portfolio. Had I looked at that property with the same goals I have now, I would have sold. The extra money upfront would have allowed me to make my next purchase on a larger building even sooner.

That's why you need to have a long-term plan beyond your initial renovation. I lost a great deal of momentum by not moving my equity, even with my refinance. Still, as I said, I have no regrets. But since I'm teaching a method here, let's look at what you can do instead.

If you buy a building for $1 million (let's say with a $300,000 down payment) and you put $200,000 into it, you're into it for $1.2 million. If you can turn around and sell it after the course of eighteen months for $1.6 million, and have a cost of sale (with the commissions and other closing costs) of $100,000, you're netting $1.5 million before you pay off your loan of $700,000.

So you're into it for $500,000 cash out of your pocket and then you sell it for $1.5 million net, so you have a $300,000 profit over the course of a year and a half. You just made a 40 percent annualized return, which is just insane when you break it down like that, especially as you can defer taxes through a 1031 exchange. If you tell people that you did a real estate fix-and-flip deal and made a low risk 40 percent annualized return, their jaws would drop.

Did yours?

We're only halfway through the book, but I just gave you the most important information you're going to find.

In fact, I'll attempt a better one. I'll summarize the whole process by telling you about a short-term flip that I actually did. In 2011, my insurance agent turned me on to a small apartment building in Pasadena. It was owned by long-term owners living on the East Coast and was managed by someone who lived far away and ran it into the ground. It had been in escrow a few times, but nobody seemed to want it, so I bought the building for $1.6 million with a $1.2 million loan, turned around and spent around $250,000 remodeling it, and sold it exactly twelve months later for $2.75 million. I turned a $400,000 down payment into an $800,000 profit in twelve months and exchanged the property into three other buildings that all had low rents and great long-term potential.

So to summarize, you find a property that is heavily devalued but with no major (structural or environmental) issues, essentially a C-grade building. You purchase it, putting a decent amount of money down so you aren't overleveraged in your loan, but with enough left in reserves for significant and *practical* renovations.

You bring the building up to a B+ or an A- (it will never be an A because it's not brand new) and you raise the rents to market level. You've just increased the value of the building and proven its market value. Now, you go to a lender or investor, get as much money as you can (either selling or refinancing, depending on your goals), and you go after the next property.

Repeat this process; don't *stop* until something in the market makes you, and slowly you will build your billion-dollar portfolio.

HOW DO YOU SELL THIS THING?

"I hold onto buildings for seven to ten years. Sometimes I'll test the market sooner if I see an impressive transaction. For example, if I bought a building and paid $200,000 per unit and noticed two years later that a similar building sold for $300,000 a unit, I may put the building on the market to see what I can get for it."

—JEFF ELOWE

I was recently discussing selling a building that a client of mine owns in Van Nuys, California. "You've seen the building; how can we clean it up before the sale?" the client asked.

My comment was, "I suggest that we take care of a few glaring items that have the appearance of deferred maintenance."

Deferred maintenance is an obvious and usually costly repair that needs to be made, such as a roof that's been patched time and time again when it really needs to be replaced. A sewer line that constantly backs up, unleashing sewage all over the courtyard. Or broken windows, a cracked sidewalk, graffiti on the garage doors, things that people can just easily see and know that a repair is needed and the owner was just too cheap or lazy and kicked the can down the road.

I can hear you shaking your book and yelling, "But Brent, didn't you say that we shouldn't focus on mechanical renovations?"

The reason I tell people to fix these issues is simple: everyone notices them and they will pay less when you go to sell or lease. Whether it's tenants—who will not pay a cent more in rent if they're overwhelmed with termites or a leaky roof—or lenders and buyers. Leaving glaring deficiencies is an easy way to be stuck with a property or sell it below market. It's an expense, for sure, but one that will fade away as you move on to new buildings and greater profits.

Investors don't mind making improvements that are going to result in obtaining a higher rent. But people mind making improvements that aren't useful in that sense. As mentioned before, tenants aren't all of a sudden going to pay a higher rent because you replaced the roof unless their specific unit has been getting roof leaks. They aren't going to pay a higher rent because you took care of a plumbing leak in one of the other units. They just aren't going to care about that.

When investors are searching for buildings to purchase, most of the savvy ones are seeking what we call "value-added opportunities." They want to spend their money making improvements that will result in a higher lease rate. So when you go to sell a building, you want to take care of obvious repairs that spook away potential buyers or cause the lenders to reduce loan amounts. If you were looking to buy a particular car, and you found out the engine needed to be replaced soon, you would probably have no interest, right? No one wants to buy a property that is going to need serious repairs the day the transaction closes.

Instead, you want them to picture how this building is going to make them money. They want to be able to put some new landscaping in, paint the exterior, make some other upgrades, and impress the prospective tenants enough when they have a vacancy to move the lease rate up.

In various cities in California, they decided that because of increased earthquake risk, they wanted all property owners to perform major upgrades to the structures of a good portion of the buildings, which were typically office and apartments. The property owners were reluctant because—as I just mentioned—none of the tenants are going to care. You're not going to get a higher rent because you just put in a steel beam in a parking garage. The city had to force the owners to make the structural repairs at their own expense.

Yet you *have* to make those upgrades. If you tried to sell a building without that structural work being completed, a potential buyer would know that they had a major bill coming as soon as the keys exchanged hands. Not to mention the worst-case scenario: If there were an earthquake, and you didn't perform the city-mandated upgrades, you'd have put your tenants at risk, you'd be facing serious liability suits, possibly criminal conviction, and your insurance likely wouldn't pay you a cent.

From the buyer's perspective, buying a building like that is problematic. You could be stuck making those improvements on your own dime, but you also have to deal with the aggravation of hiring a contractor, fronting all of the costs, going through all the city inspections, dealing with your tenants who are annoyed with the construction, et cetera. You'd rather just buy a building, turn it over to management, and let them renovate units and push the envelope to get higher rent, which most consider the fun and creative work.

PREPARING FOR THE SALE

"We've never sold a building because it's underperforming. We only sell when the time is right or for a good reason, such as the property is worth a lot more than we paid for it. We make it look good. We paint and add landscaping, for instance. If the property is in a seasonal area, we wait until the snow has all melted. If the property is in Colorado or Utah, we wait until the weather warms up."

—KEITH WASSERMAN

You want to maximize the value of the property to whatever extent you can justify.

For instance, maybe there are a few tenants in the building and their initial one-year lease is up. You can increase their rent by 5 percent and most likely no one will move out. So take a look at your rent roll and see if you have any leases rolling. If so, go ahead and let the tenant know that their rent is going up. Every dollar of extra rent results in more money when you're selling or refinancing.

Next, you want to take care of any glaring items that are going to make the building look like it's owned by a slumlord. That involves going out and taking a good look at the building. When we did a walkthrough with my client of the building in Van Nuys, we pointed out to him that there was a substantial amount of dry rot, there were wood panels that were really unattractive, and there were dead plants in the courtyard. We suggested that they perform some relatively easy upgrades that we felt would be beneficial to the value. Finally, and this is a major item, check the terms on your existing loan. Make sure that you don't have any issues with paying off your loan when you sell the building. When people purchase buildings, most obtain financing. Most commercial loans have what's called a "prepayment penalty." This is a charge that the lender imposes on the borrower (which is you as the owner/potential seller) if you pay off the loan before a certain date. It's usually a percentage of the loan amount between 1 percent and 5 percent.

If you buy a building for $4 million and you initially obtain a $2.5 million loan, the prepayment penalty might be something similar to 3 percent of the loan amount during the first and second year, 2 percent the third year, 1 percent the fourth year. If you sell the property or refinance it during the first year, the lender is going to charge you 3 percent of the balance of the loan. So on a loan of $2.5 million, that's a $75,000 expense that you're going to have to pay in order to sell the property, not including escrow, title, commissions, etc. That's a painful expense, and it's pure lost profit.

Rand Sperry says, "I've had to sell before I wanted to because I needed the money for something else. When that happened, the prepayment penalties killed me. Today, I warn buyers to avoid low-interest loans that have a large prepayment penalty if they don't think they'll be holding onto the property for a while." Banks make a fortune from investors this way.

The other thing before you sell the property, and this should be obvious, is that you'll need to find an experienced real estate broker to interview. I would suggest that you speak to two or three brokers who are knowledgeable about the specific type of property that you are considering selling and in the specific area that it's located in. If you're interested in selling an office building in Detroit, make sure you're not interviewing brokers who sell houses or apartment buildings in Chicago. Brokers have different skill sets. Residential brokers, as in the person that sold you your house, are typically not going to be a specialist for a commercial real estate transaction, but most would gladly take the listing. You need to make sure you're dealing with an expert in the types of properties in your specific market.

How do you know you've found the right broker? Have them show you what they've sold and what they have for sale. Ask for references, read up on their company, and if you want, you can check with the statewide real estate board to make sure their license is in good standing.

Find out what their marketing plan is going to be, making sure that the commission structure they want is competitive. Finally, ask their opinion on any last-minute renovations that they suggest. The broker who is going to be marketing the property should have some of the best knowledge about what needs to be done to the building pre-sale.

Danny Monempour says, "One of the biggest mistakes I made initially in my career was messing with brokers over commissions. I asked brokers for fees on deals I found to buy, which disincentivized the broker and cost me plenty of opportunities. Now, I never ask or care about how much the broker makes. I don't want to know. It's irrelevant."

I always suggest you speak to the person that sold you the property, provided that they are competent and an expert in the location and property type. Loyalty is an important thing in business. Rewarding the broker that brought you a profitable deal is a good business decision, as that broker will be incentivized to continue finding you more deals to buy in the future. Remember that deal flow, as in finding new properties to buy, is one of the most important items needed to build your portfolio and you need a team of real estate brokers finding you properties in order for you to be successful.

Lastly, a rookie move we see so many owners make is picking the broker to list their property that suggests the highest asking price and also asks for the lowest commission. That's what we call "buying the listing," and you typically end up regretting that move.

MANAGE YOUR GREED II

"It's important that the buyer feels good about the purchase. I don't like to leave too much on the table, but I will leave enough so that the buyer sees some upside and thinks he's getting a good deal."

—RAO YALAMANCHILI

When you're selling a property, there are a couple schools of thought. The school I tend to preach to people should sound familiar as I've mentioned it before in Chapter 2: manage your greed. Don't be afraid to leave a little meat on the bone for the buyer.

Meat on the bone could be a few low-rent tenants or a few improvements that a buyer can make after the purchase to increase the rent.

Now, if you're leaving something for the buyer, make sure it isn't an easy fix that could add value before the sale. In other words, for the below-market rents that you leave in the building, those should be units that are in really bad shape. Maybe it's rented out to somebody for $1,000 right now; you could probably ask $1,200, but the unit requires a large renovation first. You'd have to go and spend $20,000 on upgrades. It's a large amount of money, it's a substantial time commitment, it's a huge aggravation. Now, if you have a unit that's in really good shape, sure, raise that rent to market. Worst-case scenario is the tenant moves out and you can lease it to a new tenant for a high rent. But with a unit that's in really bad condition and the existing tenant is paying close to market, just leave it.

In one of the buildings I sold, we had eleven apartments and ten of the units we gut-renovated. I asked the property manager why we don't gut the eleventh unit. His comment was this: "That tenant is a hoarder and his unit is full of belongings. He has so much personal stuff in there it would be very hard for him to move, and probably no one would want to rent him an apartment anyways because of how much stuff he has."

They kept raising his rent to close to what they would charge if the unit was renovated and the tenant complained, but he stayed. If that tenant moved out, the unit was so disgusting that we would have had to spend $25,000 to renovate it, but instead we didn't spend a dollar. This tenant was in a situation where they really couldn't move because they had so many belongings, but we were still able to keep their unit at market value. So somebody maybe could have gotten slightly more in rent, but that would have involved having to get the tenant out and renovating the unit and dealing with all that aggravation.

Leave a few things like that for a buyer—some improvements that they can make—but take the low-hanging fruit off the table. If a unit is in great shape, raise the rent. If the unit is not in such bad shape, raise it enough that the tenant doesn't leave, and move on and sell the building. The people that are hurt trying to sell are the people who just can't give up the last dollar. Remember my client in Chapter 2 who was trying to add a rooftop deck?

However, are there aesthetic improvements that can't be ignored in preparation of a sale? Yes. If a prospective savvy investor walks into a property and it's visibly in disgusting condition, the buyer is going to assume that *everything* that they can't see is in the same poor state of disrepair. They'll assume that the plumbing is probably worse than it actually is, and the same for the roof, the windows, and the electrical. When people see poorly maintained buildings, they assume the worst, and for good reason. When people see well-maintained buildings, they assume the best. They assume that the property is in better condition than it might truly be in. Paint can hide many flaws.

It's like selling a clean, used car. If it looks good on the outside and it feels and smells good on the inside, the engine could be about to blow up, but people might not look deep enough to discover that. If someone gets into a used car and it looks and smells bad and seems poorly maintained, they're going to be much more suspicious of the condition. They are probably going to want to take the car to a mechanic and have them sort through it to make sure there are no major problems. Whereas if a car looks squeaky clean, someone might be under the impression that it's in better shape than it really is, which will mean they will be willing to overpay for it.

THE COST OF MAKING MONEY

"I sell when I have raised the rents as high as I can and any further rent increases lead to vacancies. I'll also sell if I'm having problems with the building or have a management or tenant issue. Two to three years is the longest I'll hold a property that's underperforming."

—RAO YALAMANCHILI

It's expensive to sell real estate; that's just the bottom line. If you're on a limited budget, the only way to really grow your empire is by performing some sort of exchange. You don't have to sell everything, but you sell the buildings that just don't fit your business plan anymore. Another good reason to sell is the building is too small or it's too much work to manage. Many people sell buildings because they're just plain difficult, as in management intensive and not worth the amount of work in comparison to the cash flow they receive.

It's almost as much work to manage a five-unit building as it is to manage a fifty-unit building. It's one mortgage to pay, one property tax bill to pay, one roof to fix, one sewer line to fix, and one phone call to make to verify that it's doing okay. More experienced buyers want to acquire larger buildings because of that; it is called obtaining a greater economy of scale.

When you're ready to sell, it's a good idea to pick the right time of the year. It's best to go to market at the beginning to the middle of the year. The time to not go to market is July and August when people are on vacation, as well as November and December when people just aren't paying attention. In my opinion, January to June and then maybe September and October seem to produce the best results. However, if you live in a place where there is snow on the ground from December to March, you might want to wait until it warms up. You want to put buildings on the market when buyers and brokers are at work, when kids are in school, when people are checking their emails, taking and returning phone calls and are ready for business.

Your best price comes when the highest amount of people have their eyes and attention on a new listing. You want a competitive situation where you have multiple interested buyers, so you then receive a variety of attractive offers and you can then obtain competition amongst buyers for your property. You don't want to sell your building when there's nobody looking.

Most of all, during this process, you need to listen to your broker.

Many people are just not comfortable letting someone else run the process. It's a control thing. But it's the reality of hiring a professional to handle something that needs to be done where you don't have the same level of expertise or tools. You can look at it like hiring a plumber. Sure, you can probably fix that plumbing yourself, but at what cost? You're going to most likely end up spending more for materials, and you're going to have more headaches. It's the classic time value of money philosophy: Spend your time where you make the most money.

With a broker, you're paying for the expertise, so you don't have to deal with the headache. I've worked with a number of people who just don't understand that way of thinking. "It's cheaper with my own labor." It's better to pay more money and have it done right.

HOW MUCH CAN I ASK FOR THIS?

"You have to know when to make a change internally with your team. Also, I happened to have an innate ability to determine whether something was a good deal or not. My gut instincts would tell me. The numbers had to work, of course, but I can tell a lot just by looking at a deal."

—STANLEY BLACK

One of the toughest challenges I have with clients is regarding setting the asking price for a building that they want to put on the market for sale. This is where many people struggle, and it comes down to what we discussed earlier: managing your greed. If the brokers indicate to you that your property's worth $5 million, and they suggest you put it on the market at $5.1 or $5.3 million, that's probably good advice. It's not a good idea to put it on the market at $5.5 million or more.

You're going to scare buyers off with an overly aggressive asking price. They're just not going to take it seriously. The brokers that find their clients properties to purchase will most likely completely ignore the property thinking that the seller isn't serious. People looking for properties to buy are going to say, "That deal's outrageous, that seller must not be serious, or his broker just has no idea what they're doing." You want to price the property to be competitive while it's on the market. Look at comparable properties that are currently on the market to see how they are priced, be realistic, and don't be too greedy.

Here's a true story: A client of mine has a building that he wants to sell on a street here in Los Angeles. Let's call him Ron. I advised him that the building is worth around $11 million, and that we should go to market on it at $11.25 million.

He came back and said, "I want you to put it on the market at $13.5 million."

I said, "Ron, there's just no logic to that. There's a property up the street that is nearly identical. Your building has both one- and two-bedroom units, and that building is all two-bedroom units. Your building has an income of $900,000 a year, and that building has an income of $1 million a year."

I continued, "Your building is in rough condition, and has a huge amount of obvious deferred maintenance, while that other building is beautiful and looks like somebody just renovated it this year. *That* building is on the market for $13 million and it's interestingly enough also not getting much activity from buyers. If you put your building on the market at $13.5 million, all it's going to do is make the other property look like a good deal in comparison to yours."

He still can't wrap his head around it, even though he bought the property for next to nothing, so it's all profit. Moreover, he has a legal situation with his partner and he needs to sell the building.

At an asking price of $13.5 million, he could be on the market for six months with no bites. Then he'll drop his price to $13 million, then to $12. By then, people will have seen this building listed a thousand times and figure, "Oh, not that deal again." Then he'll drop the price to $11 and finally sell it at $10.5 million.

Instead, he could save himself money and heartache by

simply finding a buyer today who is willing to pay $11 million.

That's what we call an "over-shopped" or "over-marketed" deal.

We have an expression called "chasing the market down." Another client of mine—let's call him Joe—had a building on a street called Sycamore. We listed the building for him in 2009, right as prices were falling as we were entering into the prior recession, for $2 million. An offer came in from a doctor at $1.8 million. I suggested he counter at $1.95. He countered at the full asking price. He didn't even want to give the buyer a normal contingency period or enough time to get a loan (and this was during a recession as well), and not surprisingly, that buyer disappeared.

It was 2009, prices were dropping, and Joe had just turned down an offer at $1.8 and the buyer probably would have paid $1.9. A month later, we received an offer at $1.7. By then, we had reduced the price, dropping the property to $1.95 million.

We countered this buyer at $1.9. (This was two months after our first original offer at $1.8 million.) The new buyer said, "I'll pay $1.75." Joe wouldn't take it, and again the buyer disappeared.

One month after that, an offer came in at $1.7 million. Joe

countered at $1.9, the buyer agreed to pay $1.8, and we sold the property. Joe could have sold the property for $1.9 three months earlier, but instead he couldn't manage his greed when the market was dropping and refused to sell at a market price.

Later, after the sale, I asked, "Joe, what was driving your decision-making at the time?"

He responded, "You know, I just wasn't comfortable to pull the trigger. I just felt that I needed it to be on the market for longer, and I was hoping somebody would come and pay my price, because I've been so used to getting my price. Every time I sold a building, I would get my price."

The mistake that we made, the mistake that *I* made, was that of the other buildings I was selling, the market—and therefore the value of the property—was improving while the building was on the market. Maybe I put the property on the market for $2 million at a time it was only worth $1.8. But six months later by the time escrow closed, it was worth $1.9 or more, so I felt like I was a genius selling it for that price.

Hindsight's always 20/20, right? People always look back on the things they did and realize they made an obvious, glaring mistake, but at the time they were making the best decisions they could.

All too often, people become caught up in the greed of trying to take a massive profit instead of just executing on their original business plan.

I tell people, your best offers usually come in the first few weeks after marketing has commenced. Those are usually from active buyers who are actually out there looking, and they're aggressive. If you don't take those initial offers, it could come back to haunt you when nobody else shows up later.

When you prepare to sell a property, you need to have a plan of what you're going to want to purchase next. Not necessarily the actual building but the property type and general location. Maybe you want to buy a larger building in the same area. Maybe you want to sell an apartment building and buy an office building. If you want to buy an office building, how big and what market do you want to be in? You need to have some sort of plan. You don't want to be figuring this out two months later.

Before you put your property on the market for sale, you should already be in the process of looking for the next one to buy for a few reasons. The first is that you'll need confidence in your ability to find a suitable exchange property for the one you are selling. The second is there needs to be a way for you to find the next property, and you can start by talking to brokers, letting people know you're in the market, and asking them to help you find something to buy. If you intend to keep your momentum, that's one of the most important things. That's how some of my clients buy twenty buildings in a year. They just don't stop looking for the next deal to buy.

HANDLING HARDSHIP

"I see a potential problem when multiple tenants have moved into a building at about the same time. That means you'll probably have major turnover at some point. This could become an ordeal because you'll need to re-lease a lot of your units around the same time, hurting your cash flow. It's worse if you have to hold units vacant for renovations."

—PAUL LING

The market is cyclical, but that doesn't mean you won't be surprised when there is a drastic turn. In 2019, a virus sprang up in Asia and quickly traveled around the world. The COVID-19 coronavirus became a viscous pandemic in the space of a few months. In three months, the United States went from zero confirmed cases to over 6.2 million, with over 220,000 deaths.

As you can imagine, this led to a number of unexpected changes to every single commercial real estate market. Many states ordered their residents to shelter in place, and non-essential businesses were shut down and the unemployment rate skyrocketed to 20 percent in major cities. For the real estate industry, things became very tense quickly. I had to deal with not only worried clients, but my own buildings as well. Fortunately, this wasn't the first time I'd had to weather a financial storm, and I had learned some valuable lessons.

A good client of mine named William bought a couple of apartment buildings in 2005 and 2006. When the recession hit in 2009, one of his investor's came to him and said, "We need to sell the building that I invested in with you as I need to get my cash out."

William said, "It's not a good time to sell for the rest of the partners as we bought it for $2 million and it's probably worth less than $1.8 right now. We'd be losing money."

The investor came clean and said that the recession unexpectedly put him in a difficult situation. He had an issue arise and he desperately needed cash.

William said, "We're not going to sell the property at a loss; however, your initial investment in the property was $50,000. I'll go talk to all the investors and I'll see if anyone's willing to just buy your ownership interest. But you need to understand that if the building is worth $1.8 million, your $50,000 initial investment is now worth more like $35,000 based on the current value of the property."

It was a recession, nobody had any money sitting in their savings accounts, and people who did have money were afraid to spend it. None of the investors were interested in buying him out.

The investor was becoming desperate, and at that point William said, "If you really need to get out, I can purchase your position, but I'm only going to give you $10,000."

The investor responded, "That's less than what I need and less than what it's worth, but if you can make it $15,000 I would consider it." They cut a deal and William bought him out for literally 30 cents on the dollar. It was a business deal. The investor needed the money, and none of the other investors wanted to sell the building at a loss. It is one of the downfalls of being an investor in an asset that you don't control as well as not having enough cash on reserve to endure a crisis.

During the pandemic of 2020, we also witnessed a few similar deals go down. People needed money, the market was still correcting, and investors took losses in the stock market—including me—just to have some cash in hand. I won't tell you that it makes it easier when you know the hit is coming, but you can take comfort in knowing that there is a path forward when the dust settles.

1031 EXCHANGE IN PRACTICE

"When I sold my second building, I planned to do an exchange. But I couldn't find an exchange property that I liked and I eventually had to pay taxes on the sale."

—RAO YALAMACHILI

When you sell a property, you have two choices: Cash out of the investment, which means paying taxes on any gain, or perform a 1031 Exchange.

Cashing out is the act of not reinvesting the money. Let's say you bought a retail property for $1 million, and a few years later, you sold it for $2 million and you want to get out of the real estate business and you're just calling it a day. You will pay taxes on the profit, but you're okay with that situation because you made such an enormous profit.

The second option is what is called a 1031 Exchange. As I mentioned earlier in Chapter 2, it's the IRS tax code 1031. If you bought a retail property for $1 million and you sold it for $2 million, you have around a $1 million capital gain (not including depreciation, but your accountant will need to figure out all of the details for you). As long as you reinvest the money under the IRS guidelines, you defer your taxes for a later date. When you sell that next property, you can also exchange out of it, or you can cash out and pay taxes on both the first sale as well as the second.

When the property you sold closes escrow, you have six months from the date it closes until the date that you close escrow on the building you're going to buy. If you don't close by then, or you didn't fulfill the other fairly straight-forward guidelines, the IRS can theoretically say that you didn't fulfill your 1031 Exchange and you owe taxes on the property you sold.

The other requirement is to replace all the capital, the proceeds from the sale. For example, let's say the building that you sold was $2 million and it had a $1.3 million loan on it, you had $100,000 in closing costs (commissions, escrow, title, etc.) so you pulled out $600,000 in cash after the sale. The next property you buy has to be the same or greater in three categories: purchase price (at least $2 million), loan amount (at least a $1.3 million loan), and lastly you need to reinvest all of the money that you netted (the $600,000). You'll need to have all of the funds go through a third party intermediary, which we call a 1031 accommodator, which your escrow company or real estate broker can assist you in finding.

PURCHASE PRICE

The property that you buy has to be valued at least $2 million (the same price or greater than the property that you just sold). You can purchase more than one property.

LOAN AMOUNT

The loan you take out against the new property has to be the same or greater than the $1.3 million loan you had on the property you sold.

REINVEST ALL PROCEEDS

Lastly, you have to reinvest every dollar you pull out. If you sell the building for $2 million and, after all your costs, you pull out $600,000, you need to place every last dollar into the next property that you own. That is the guideline for a 1031 Exchange. Of course, if the property you want to purchase requires more than $600,000, you can put in additional funds.

The IRS intends for you to purchase property of the same or larger value, and they want you to not pull any cash out. They don't want you to pocket any of the proceeds. The goal is for you to reinvest all of the proceeds.

Now, a couple things to note: One, as mentioned above, you don't have to buy just one property, you can buy two, three, four or more, as long as the value adds up to at least what you sold the property for. The second thing is you could purchase a property for a lower sales price than what is required, but you will pay taxes on what we call the "boot."

Boot is the amount of money that you don't reinvest, and you'll just end up paying taxes on that amount. You could sell a building for $2 million and go buy another building for $1 million. The IRS will say that you didn't reinvest all the funds, so you owe partial capital gains tax on the portion of the sale that you didn't utilize. The important thing is for you to check with your accountant to find out exactly what your tax exposure will be for whatever investment plan you enter into.

BUILDING A REAL ESTATE EMPIRE

"My biggest mistake early on was trying to manage buildings myself. Managing the buildings took me away from the more lucrative job of finding new properties to purchase. It was like trading a $50-an-hour job for the $5-an-hour job of managing apartment buildings."

—RAND SPERRY

If you manage your sales effectively and make smart renovations, these investments can make you a significant profit. The return on real estate at this scale can be incredibly lucrative, but maybe that's not your plan.

Some people are satisfied with owning one or two commercial properties. Some people want to have ten or twenty office buildings, shopping centers or apartment buildings. A rare few have the drive to build a portfolio valued at a billion dollars, owning hundreds of buildings. So how can you get there?

First, learn from my mistakes and the mistakes of many of my clients. Make the renovations and repairs that make sense, and either put them on the market to sell at a realistic price or refinance the properties, pull some cash out, and reinvest the proceeds. While I was able to turn some lemons into a small amount of fairly sour lemonade out of my first major commercial real estate investment, that's not the method I want you to try on your own purchases.

When you're ready to sell, do the legwork. Shop for a good broker, conduct your research, and *listen* to them. Finally, always be on the lookout for your next property.

At a certain point in your career, you're going to have so many buildings that it grows harder and harder to keep track of them all. At that point, your success rides on your ability to properly delegate responsibility.

You're then going to need a good property management company. Unfortunately, those are a bit harder to navigate.

CHAPTER 5

_____

MANAGING YOUR TIME, YOUR MONEY, YOUR PROPERTY

"Over time, I've built my own team. I have worked with property management companies in the past, and with shopping centers, leasing is a big challenge. In apartment buildings, the big challenge is repairs and maintenance."

—ANDREW TAVAKOLI

A few years back, I had a client named John, who had a serious problem. His renovation project turned into a lawsuit he'd filed on one of his ex-employees.

John owned retail properties throughout the country but was moving his portfolio into apartments and was in the process of renovating a fifty-unit apartment building that I helped him purchase. He had a property management company handling the lion's share of the ongoing responsibility, but John was a meticulous owner. He liked to be involved, especially in endeavors with this large of a renovation budget.

At some point, John sat down and looked over the last few months of the expenses for the renovations and noticed that they were drastically higher than he'd anticipated. He checked and then double checked his estimates, but something wasn't adding up. Part of the project was replacing all of the windows. His employee had ordered 200 windows and that didn't sound right, so he drove down to the building to see for himself. He walked around the property and counted windows himself, arriving at closer to 150.

John asked around and discovered the problem. His employee had ordered extra windows with the goal of using them to renovate her own house, of course without John's knowledge. He then noticed that other things didn't add up and additional materials were ordered that weren't used at his property, most likely at his employee's house, which he later found out was fully renovated at the same time. Considering the fraud involved, John had to file a lawsuit to try and recoup that financial loss.

Whether you're buying five buildings or fifty, you don't have the bandwidth to serve as both real estate investor, property manager, and construction supervisor. At some point in your career, if you truly plan on building a billion dollar portfolio, you're going to have to employ at least one property management company. No matter how much vetting you do, there will come a time when you discover some manner of malfeasance in the operations.

CHECK YOUR POCKETS

"The biggest challenge is finding the right trusted contractor who knows what to do."

—JERRY FINK

As a real estate attorney once told me: It's not a question of whether or not your property management company is stealing from you, it's a question of *how much* they're stealing.

Unless you self-manage, you have to hire people to take care of the property for you, and those people or the people that they hire are most likely dipping into the cookie jar. I remember the story of a maintenance worker who collected money from laundry machines. When he emptied the tumbler of quarters, he dumped 90 percent into a bag headed to the owner's bank, and the other 10 percent went into his pockets. It may not seem like a big deal to steal five bucks at a time, but with five or ten buildings over the course of a year, the guy robbed a couple thousand dollars annually.

It's a little easier to catch people who take actual objects. The supervisor that's lifting extra material after a renovation project tends to be caught eventually. It gets more difficult when you have employees padding time or inflating projects.

Take the contractor who bills you for work that he didn't actually do. He shows up for an hour to fix a plumbing leak, but he bills you for two hours. Or he has some leftover parts in his truck from another job, but he bills you or someone else for materials anyways. This happens all the time. It's double dipping, it's fraud, but it's done in a nickel-and-dime manner. Most owners don't even know it's happening.

I had a building that needed to be maintained, so it was recommended by management that I should pay $100 per week for someone to weekly clean the trash from the common areas. Every time I went to the property, it was disgusting; there was trash everywhere. I confronted my property manager about the situation and he told me it was because of the school down the block. The kids supposedly would hang out and leave their trash.

I went out there once during the summer, when school was out, and there was still trash everywhere. All the red flags started waving and I started investigating. Turns out I was being robbed. The property management company never hired anyone to clean the property; they were just charging me and pocketing the $100 per week cleaning charge.

COWBOYS AND SHERIFFS

"I have stressful days that prompt me to say, 'I'm done.' But I enjoy waking up in the morning knowing I have a million things to accomplish. I enjoy playing the game—it's fun, crazy, and your success is not guaranteed, and this motivates me. I also enjoy seeing younger people learn the business. I'm mentoring some of them and watching them start their careers, and I get a lot of satisfaction from that."

—JERRY FINK

According to Don Hendricks—who founded Hendricks and Partners, which was later sold to Berkadia—in the commercial real estate industry, there are two types of personalities: cowboys and sheriffs. The cowboys are the gun-slinging sales guys who are out in the field calling property owners, prospecting, and putting deals together. They're not necessarily attention-detailed, but they are the rainmakers. They are out finding new business, putting transactions together, and they then turn over all the details to the sheriffs.

The sheriffs are the organized, methodical people, who are more focused and able to get all the details right. Most of the really successful owners I've worked with are what I would call cowboys. They are simply just out slinging deals, meeting people, talking on the phone, and they then turn over the detailed work to their team of sheriffs. That would be their property management team, accounting, leasing, legal, or their maintenance staff.

It's a critical puzzle. You need to have the right people in the right positions to make the machine work. If you're great at talking to people, negotiating deals, seeking out the next deal to buy, then why would you pay someone else to take that work off your plate? It's arguably the most rewarding and exciting part of the business. If you are a cowboy, then you don't want anyone else taking the lead. Still, you need sheriffs to keep your business running.

There was an amazingly successful client of mine named Jeff. He is a billionaire, a Forbes 100, who ran for governor in a recent election. He is one of the most amazing deal-makers I've ever seen. I remember going to his office and sitting in a room waiting with five other people scheduled to see him. He'd see you for five or ten minutes, then they'd shoo you out. If you called him, a secretary or receptionist would answer and ask you to stay on hold, and she was just lining up calls for him. He'd take one call, "Hi, who are you? What do you need? What do you have for me to buy? It sounds like a good deal, send me over all the info. Thanks." CLICK. Then you'd email him the information. They'd look at it, and if he was interested, he or someone from his office would call you back and have you write the offer. Talk about efficiency!

He was taking probably thirty phone calls an hour, just having very quick, short conversations with people, then he'd turn over the rest to his team, who would handle making sure the purchase agreement and eventual transaction were done right.

Jeff was entirely focused on buying apartment buildings at the time, but he had zero interest in property management, and consequently his buildings suffered. He ended up landing in trouble with the City of Los Angeles because he just wasn't paying attention to maintaining the buildings. To him, that wasn't a priority. The oversight cost him, and though he has managed to keep moving and growing his empire, think of all the trouble and expense he could have saved with the help of a good team of sheriffs.

I tell people that you can't just focus on one thing, but you can scale your business by hiring people to focus on the areas that you don't feel are worth your time. There are only so many hours in the day. So when it comes to managing your costs and time, property management is one of the most effective ways to scale your business.

Most people don't have enough buildings that they can afford to hire their own staff. The cost of hiring your own maintenance person, accounting person, leasing person, and putting everybody on payroll, is between $250,000 and $400,000 a year. That's just for three or four quality people. Whereas, you could hire a property management company and just pay them a small percentage of the income of the buildings.

YOU CAN'T DO THIS ALONE

"I owned some properties in New York and had to hire a management company. The biggest challenge is not the 5 percent you have to pay, but the 15 percent inefficiency of the management company. I learned that it's better to give ulcers than to receive them."

—FRED LEEDS

Here's your quote of the day: No one became a billionaire by cleaning their own toilets.

No matter how hands-on you tend to be in other aspects of life, you need to learn to delegate to succeed in the real estate business. Unfortunately, it's going to open you up to some risk.

I wish I could tell you that there is an easy way to avoid being ripped off. Sadly, that is just a reality of this business. You will work with some amazing, honorable people, and you'll work with others you'll hope to never run into again. That's true of every industry in existence but especially in real estate where the stakes are so high. It's best if you prepare yourself for this eventuality rather than letting it blindside you.

Maybe you think you can avoid this if you manage all the properties yourself. That may work if you own one or two properties, but you'll be overwhelmed by the time you hit ten. The reality is, even if you are robbed a little bit, that's what we call the cost of doing business. You will eventually grow your business by delegating, by spreading yourself out and focusing on the things that make you money. The things that make you the most money are finding the next deal to buy and adding value to your existing properties so you can then refinance and pull cash out for the next deal or sell them for a profit.

That's why delegation is one of the most important skills you can learn. Delegation is all about specificity and trust. You have to give clear, precise instructions, and then trust that those are going to be carried out. But watch out—and remember what Ronald Reagan said—you have to "trust, but verify." If you aren't periodically spot-checking the work of your managers, you're asking for them to take advantage of you.

Another foolish thing is to attempt to sell the property yourself. You consider the potential commission you would have to pay and say, "I don't want to pay a broker $100,000. How can I avoid that expense? Can I try to sell it myself?" That might find you in a lawsuit and most likely undersell the property.

A real estate purchase involves an enormous amount of legal paperwork. If you make a mistake on a contract, it can cost you and your investors more money in the end than it was worth. While it might be tempting to try and save that $100,000, it is simply not worth it in the long run. Instead, save yourself the weeks of headache and hassle. Trust in the professionals. The time and energy you save are worth far more than the commission.

I have a client named Larry who owned a commercial building in Malibu. Larry was thinking of selling the property, and before he could make a decision regarding hiring a broker, he was inundated with offers. A buyer contacted him directly, and it seemed logical for him to respond to the offer with a counter offer. Larry decided that he would do this himself rather than involve a broker so he could avoid paying a commission. Unfortunately, Larry made an error in the counter offer that he prepared on his own and the buyer accepted it at a price of around $250,000 less than what Larry intended, and of course the buyer wasn't willing to walk away as he knew better. Larry may have saved $100,000 on commission, but he undersold the property by far more.

As you build your portfolio, eventually you are going to need to build a small coalition of people to help you achieve your goals. From property managers and brokers to a network of skilled technicians, you need to hire and control a large number of people. As you scale up even more, you'll entrust a smaller group to then manage the people underneath them. It's like any business; you're just scaling it and establishing the chain of command.

So how should you decide when to hire new employees?

HIRING SPREE

"I always outsource property management. Although I can run a $9 billion portfolio with a team of fifty-two people, it's not always practical to manage these properties yourself. I'd need 520 people to do that. What are the biggest challenges when working with property management? If the staffing is weak, untrained, and unmotivated, you're dead."

—BOB HART

It comes down to two things: 1) The cost of hiring employees, and 2) economy of scale.

If you own three apartment buildings that are each twenty units, you're never going to be able to justify the cost of having a full-time employee. For example, if a basic employee who could help you with property management charges you $20 an hour, that is close to $45,000 per year. If you factor in all of the other costs associated with payroll and taxes, that's costing you closer to $55,000 per year.

You're better off hiring a management company because you don't yet have an economy of scale large enough to justify this expense. While there are certainly outliers, most property management companies will charge a percentage of the building's revenue, usually around 5 percent. In any case, that is probably more cost effective than a full-time employee at this stage of the game.

Now, if you increase to a hundred units or more, you justify the expense of hiring one full-time person to be your property supervisor. You'll need to conduct your due diligence and a solid background check with references, but this one employee is going to work out better than siphoning off more and more to a management company.

This causes trouble for some real estate investors. They expect this new employee to be a jack of all trades. In reality, this person is likely going to be good at one or two things. Maybe they can do plumbing and basic maintenance, but they aren't great with people and often forget to collect rent. Or they're organized and reliable but only know bookkeeping.

I've seen people successfully run their small operation with one person, but that person is just not good at more than half the things the owner needs them to do. Often, in these cases, the owner starts to micromanage. And once they start, it usually gets worse. First, they'll supervise collecting rent, then they want updates on maintenance, then they need to walk the grounds. Soon, they're doing their full-time employee's job.

It ends up taking more time out of their life than before they hired their employee. They just can't give up that control and that power. I have to preach to people that for them to grow, they're going to have to give up control.

That starts with entrusting a small group of people to handle the day-to-day operations of your buildings. As you continue to grow, you'll need to scale even more. You'll hire staff to run a collection of buildings, advising you on renovations and maybe even seeking out brokers on your behalf. You'll have acquisitions staff scouring the country for new properties to purchase, though you should always be the final authority on that matter.

As your portfolio grows larger and larger, so, too, will your team. If you've hired wisely and weeded out the ones that weren't a good fit, you'll find yourself working with a trusted group of advisors and helpers.

BUILDING A TEAM

"I hired a helper, then a bookkeeper, and then some maintenance people. I added more people as I needed them for the properties I own close to my home. However, I hired property management firms for properties I've purchased in other cities."

—DAVID SOUFER

There are a number of priorities in building your own crew. What are your needs? What are your goals? Are there services in your area that are just too expensive to hire out piecemeal? Again, it comes down to economy of scale.

If you have hundreds of units and commercial space, you can afford to hire a full-time plumber, maintenance worker, bookkeeping, and leasing agent. You could even have a few people on staff to assist those employees.

Notice that this list doesn't cover everything. You have to call some sort of a specialist at one point or another. If you have a roofing problem, you're going to have to call a roofer. If your elevator or fire alarm system needs maintenance, that type of repair requires specialized training and licensing. Unless you have so many buildings that you can afford to have every single type of trade on staff, you're going to have to subcontract out some of the work, including renovations.

Danny Monempour developed his own team to handle property management. He claims he had no choice as, "Management companies won't turn properties. They won't do asset management." Which means that most management companies will simply pay the bills but won't actively work to improve the property and reposition it to sell or refinance at a profit.

As we said earlier, the management company will typically charge you around 5 percent of the income of the property for smaller buildings and a lower percentage for larger buildings. So if the property generates $200,000 in annual income, they're going to charge you $10,000. If you have ten buildings like that, the property management company just charged you $100,000. And for that amount of money, you can probably afford to go hire one or two people and handle things in-house. But if you hire people, you're going to have to put them in an office somewhere, and you're going to have to give them employee benefits and put them on payroll.

Building a team also comes with new responsibilities and new challenges. You have to consider liability employment risk. The amount of employment-related lawsuits in the last decade has gone staggeringly up. Property owners and management companies are an easy target for employment lawsuits.

That's another reason why people prefer not to manage their own buildings. If there is an issue with your management company, you can fire them and hire another one. If the issue is because of one of your employees, all of a sudden you're responsible for them. It's much easier to fire a property management company than to fire an employee.

However, you have more control of the team you build in-house. If you don't like the plumber that your management company uses, that's just too bad. They only have the one person, and they're not firing him over one unsatisfied building owner. While it is a bit more paperwork and hassle to fire your own employee, you can more easily remove non-performers and find a new trade worker.

If you decide to build your own team, there will still come a day when you discover that one of your employees has made an enormous mistake. In the best-case scenario, they made an honest mistake and you can work with them to fix it and hopefully you can forge a stronger relationship with your worker and end up with better long-term performance.

The worst-case scenario is that they did something illegal, either to you or to a tenant. In that instance, you'll have no choice but to take action. It won't be fun, and it will cost money if you have to hire an attorney, but you can't allow that sort of behavior to continue.

So how can you protect yourself and catch these problems before they metastasize? "Trust, but verify." If you're delegating properly, but never checking in on your properties, you're asking to be taken for a ride. You need to go down to your buildings every once in a while and actually look around. If you have a major renovation, you need to be involved. This isn't an easy, hands-off business. The billion dollar portfolio doesn't just build itself. You need to be willing to put in the hard work in order to get the best results.

THE MOST IMPORTANT EMPLOYEE

"I noticed a big improvement when I hired an operational expert. The expert hired regional managers for my properties and this helped me grow my business. It's critical to have good onsite representatives. If you don't have the right people, it's a real issue."

—JEFF ELOWE

Of all the employees watching over your property, you will have the closest relationship with your property supervisor. You need to have a point person. This is one person you can call that knows what's going on with all the buildings you own.

The property supervisor knows of the maintenance issues, what repairs need to be made, and who is fixing what. They can tell you which tenants haven't paid rent, or what's the plan to evict them or get them caught up on back rent. They know what units are and will be vacant, and what renovations they have planned. They know what units are currently for rent and how many people have inquired and applied. You want to have one person that handles all of these items.

Can you imagine all those phone calls you'd have to make to find out the facts of each of those items if you had various employees handling different tasks at different buildings? That's hours of your day per building you own. You want to have one person who knows all the answers and empower them to call the leasing company, the plumber, or the roofer. They need to meet with the bookkeeper or the accountant who's handling the rents received. If you have one person who can handle all of this, you don't have to deal with it. You can make one or two phone calls a day to that person and receive an update on everything.

Income properties are supposed to be passive investments. A passive investment is one that does not require your full-time attention. It's not supposed to be the equivalent of running a business like supermarkets where you have hundreds of employees and tens of thousands of customers. Those are active businesses. However, commercial real estate investments only become passive when you have a good enough property management company or a good enough property supervisor that can take responsibility over all those matters, so you don't have to.

This needs to be a trusted employee. You'll likely go through several property supervisors before you find the person that fits your style. It's a relationship, and you'll be putting in work to develop them until things click. Once they understand the business, your calendar opens up dramatically. Suddenly, you can focus on the bigger picture and let the supervisor keep your properties running smoothly.

Try to picture yourself at the end of this road. You own hundreds of buildings amounting to a massive portfolio.

How much is your time worth per hour? $500? $1,000? $10,000? Why are you spending so much time doing the $15 per hour tasks? That is why you delegate, because your time is worth too much to spend on the everyday tasks. You have to be focused on the big picture of growing your business. It's not that these tasks aren't important, or that the people doing them aren't important, but that your job is to focus elsewhere.

When you start out, you should probably hire property management for your first few buildings. I suggest this for two reasons: 1) you don't know enough about the business, and 2) it's just not worth trying to figure out how to write leases, how to find a plumber, how to find a roofer, how to handle dealing with evictions and city inspections, and so on.

When you own two or three buildings, maybe you want to perform some of the work yourself, because at this point you're more experienced. But in order to be able to scale your business and go from owning five buildings to fifty, you're going to have to delegate and turn over day-to-day tasks that are not critical to scaling your business. The biggest, most time-consuming aspect is simply property management.

THE RAINY DAY FUND

"I tend to buy during a down cycle. During the recession in the

1990s, a fifth of my buildings were upside down and I had to make arrangements with my banks to save them."

—RAO YALAMANCHILI

Even with a solid property management company, you need to routinely check in on your properties. Remember that this is your name, your reputation, and your money on the line. If something happens at the building, the buck stops with you.

As previously mentioned, Jeff had one of his buildings red flagged by the city because of multiple code violations. It was in a state of incredible disrepair because it wasn't being managed properly. While he was living out of state, he hired a property management company to handle his California portfolio. The company was constantly calling him, asking to fund the property to pay for the repairs, and he just wasn't interested in focusing any of his financial resources there.

It's one thing to have a property management company, it's another thing to be making sure they're doing their job. You can't just completely turn everything over to a property management company without having some oversight. There might be times when the building needs a $100,000 repair, but there's only $20,000 left in the bank account for that property. You're going to have to pull money from somewhere else to take care of your business.

Emergencies come up, and you need to maintain some sort of a slush fund, or a rainy day fund, to pay for big ticket items. You could wake up one day to learn a hurricane wiped out half your building. You can't wait for the insurance to come in and pay for it; you're going to need to start spending money to take care of a disaster. You could be in California and there could be an earthquake that damages the building. There could be a plumbing or roofing disaster and the building gets flooded. In any case, you're going to need to come up with money very quickly to take care of that problem. Because if you don't, you're going to have a bigger problem on your hands.

The people that don't carry cash reserves to take care of those problems are not making a wise decision as it will eventually come back to haunt them. There will always be another challenge on the horizon. There might come a time when rents drop, or the economy tanks, or a global pandemic leads to rent freezes or even strikes. When your building isn't making as much money as it was before, you're going to have a hard time paying the bills. If you're overleveraged with no cash reserves, you're going to suffer. If you have huge loans on the property and the income drops substantially, you're going to be in bad shape as you'll need to be feeding the building from your savings account to keep it above water. It is critical in this business to keep some reserve money around.

From my experience, it's best to keep around $500 per unit on reserves at any given time to pay for anything that might unexpectedly come up. Lenders often want 5 percent of a buyer's net worth to be in liquid assets for this purpose in stocks, cash, etc.

When you're in the process of purchasing a property and working on a loan, the lender is also going to verify that you have money for this rainy day fund. If the lender asks, "Where's all your equity from?" and you say, "I have exactly enough for the down payment for the building I want to purchase in my savings account," they might become concerned. The lender wants to make sure you have some reserves—maybe another 10 percent, another $100,000. It depends on the lender's requirements. Lenders often want 5 percent of a buyer's net worth or the equivalent of twelve months of property taxes, insurance, principal, and interest to be in liquid reserves such as cash, bonds, or stocks.

For example, during Christmas 2018, an apartment building that I own flooded as a result of a catastrophic roof leak and we had no choice but to spend $300,000 repairing it over the course of the following six months. These things can happen at any time.

ECONOMY OF SCALE

"I manage the properties myself with our staff unless it's a head-ache. In that case, I hire someone else to handle it."

—DAVID POURBABA

"I always hire management companies. Still, I visit every property I own at least once a month so I can collect the change from onsite laundry machines and keep an eye on it."

—PAUL LING

There is a recurring theme in almost all businesses. A store owner can't run ten stores by themselves. They are going to have to hire people and turn it over to management. A chain restaurant owner can't manage every location personally. They need to hire and train talented supervisors underneath them. It's the same exact principle with real estate, and it's a substantial challenge. Most people originally became successful in business because—in their minds—they were hands-on, doing everything their way and doing it themselves.

To turn it over to third-party management is a psychological nightmare for some people. They're worried about low-level employees stealing from them, incompetence, or they're just worried that somebody isn't going to do it right (as in the way *they* would do it). You will certainly encounter this feeling, but it can be overcome. To grow your business, you must admit that it will not be possible for you to accomplish everything yourself.

The first building I purchased? I was completely freaked out. Where am I going to find tenants? How am I going to make repairs? How am I going to deal with the city? What happens when I have a vacancy? Who's going to renovate the unit?

It was an overwhelming and daunting concern. I realized that I needed to hire a property management company and have them perform all of the work. Then it all seemed to make sense. If I was concerned with the job they were doing, I could become as involved as I felt necessary and I certainly had the resources to find solutions to problems.

That's what it takes to expand. You won't achieve a high level of success in this business if you can't separate caution and fear. Having some oversight can go a long way toward keeping you calm and collected while delegating. Another client of mine uses property management companies, but then also hires a company to audit the property management company's books.

The property management company manages his buildings on a day-to-day basis, and a monthly report is sent to the owner by an auditing company that looks it over. If they see a large repair, they ask to see the bills. They want to find out why it was made. They want to make sure there was a competitive bid and that the repairs were completed.

Yes, it costs more money to have an audit company look

over the books, but the presumption is that this keeps the property management company more aimed at being efficient and cost effective, as well as honest. Please always remember: "Trust but verify."

IT'S ABOUT THE BIGGER PICTURE

"We always hire a third party. At first, we tried to do it ourselves, but it bogged us down. It prevented growth. Also, we are in too many markets to do it ourselves. Property management is a low-margin business to begin with."

—KEITH WASSERMAN

If you're able to delegate property management away from your own hands, you will have more time, energy, and resources to focus on the big picture of growing your business. Your one priority each morning when you wake up needs to be, "How can I buy more buildings?" When you start your day, you should not be thinking about, "How do I take care of this plumbing problem? How do I take care of the city inspection? How do I deal with training the new employee that we just hired?" You need to acquire more buildings, and everything else should be delegated to someone else to handle.

The only way you're ever going to be successful is by focusing on one thing, like a professional athlete would do. Picture a pro-player in the NBA. He wakes up every day and thinks about improving his game. He might also be a television personality or have his own clothing line, but that's his second job, and he has other people dealing with those businesses.

His main concerns are training, going to the gym, shooting hoops, and just improving his game. He has trainers and coaches, but becoming a better player is his job, his focus, and top priority. Everything else takes a back seat and is handled by people that he hires.

A very good client of mine, Michael Sorochinsky, started out as an attorney. He invested in a small apartment building in West Hollywood and caught the bug. Later, he bought another, and it snowballed from there. When he sold those early investments, he bought larger buildings and took on institutional investors. He was moving so much property that he became friendly with a handful of brokers.

Eventually, he realized that the best way for him to have access to inventory of the types of buildings that he was targeting to purchase was to continue to become really tight with the brokers. So he came to the conclusion that he could open up his own brokerage company and bring in these brokers to work in-house, helping him to find more deals to buy and having them resell the properties later. So a handful of brokers came in and worked for Michael in his office where they continued to find him great deals to buy. Michael then renovated the buildings, pushed the rents, and gave his brokers back the properties to sell at a higher price.

They created a business model of buying value-added commercial and apartment buildings, renovating them to various degrees, raising rents, and then selling them for a profit. He scaled his business quickly and hired a property management company to handle the daily aspects of running the institutional quality buildings, but eventually he grew so large that he had to bring in more help. He built a family operation and uses a third-party team to manage the mundane tasks, leaving him to his favorite aspects of the business. He spends his days working with his investors, putting deals together, and enjoying his personal and financial success.

I tell people that if they own five buildings and they are considering bringing on a third-party management company, they should go ahead and hire a company to handle one of the buildings in your portfolio. Take the building that is the farthest away, the most challenging and time consuming for you, where you have the worst issues with items like repairs and tenants and turn it over to a management company. If after around six months you're happy with the work that they are doing, then maybe turn over all the buildings to that company or turn over another building and just see how it goes.

You're never going to become a billionaire by micromanaging and handling everything yourself. You are only going to reach that goal by hiring other people, so you can scale your business.

MANAGING YOUR EXPECTATIONS

"I prefer to manage my properties with my own team. It's not about saving money, however. For me, it's about control and being able to watch the pulse. When I'm managing my own properties, I know the trends in rents, where tenants are moving to, if there is more crime in the area, or if police presence is increased. This is vital information for me."

—RAO YALAMANCHILI

In order to build that billion dollar portfolio, it's obvious that you need to buy a ton of buildings, and it's important that you focus on acquiring buildings that are not going to be management disasters. It is going to be challenging if you are purchasing buildings that run like hotels where tenants are constantly moving in and out. You are probably going to want to avoid purchasing buildings that you feel are going to require constant and expensive ongoing repairs, where the city is going to constantly be ordering you to fix this and that, where you're going to have long-term issues with tenants. Commercial properties are even more challenging as it's so much more costly to lease office and retail space as there are leasing commission and tenant improvement budgets. Lastly, it takes much longer to fill a vacancy in these properties.

In order to have the time and space to find those buildings and make those business decisions, you need to delegate responsibility. Some people have multiple property management companies depending on where the property is located. Some owners have management companies that handle their class A buildings and others that handle their class C buildings. Some management companies might excel in one market but are less experienced and efficient in the next market over.

If you decide to hire your own staff, be prepared to become immersed in staffing and personnel management. If you don't have an HR department, then guess what? You are the human resources department. Run background checks, ask for references, and look over and inspect the work you ask your employees to handle.

Soon, you'll have a trusted group of management companies or personal property supervisors. You'll have a few phone numbers that you can dial to find out everything you need to know about your business. At that moment, you need to keep your momentum going. Maybe you own a few dozen buildings—and that is quite an accomplishment—but we're not done yet.

As you grow, you might suddenly struggle to find new properties to purchase. You might need to become much more flexible than you had originally planned as your criteria will need to evolve.

CHAPTER 6

———

ASSET CLASSES AND DIVERSIFICATION

"I wish I had acquired other asset classes, such as office and industrial properties."

—JEFF ELOWE

In 2011, California Bank & Trust hired us to sell a portfolio of fifteen apartment buildings that they had foreclosed on. Around eight of them were in Long Beach, and the rest were in Riverside, California. We took the listings, marketed them all, and successfully sold the buildings, but there's always a story behind properties.

All of these buildings previously were owned by one group, who lost the properties through the foreclosure process.

These were "REO" properties, which stands for "real estate owned," in other words, owned by a bank or another institution. Banks aren't in the business of owning foreclosed properties, so they try to sell them one way or another.

We found out that the borrower had a very typical story. Originally, they started buying small apartment buildings in Long Beach and then expanded by going east and buying buildings in the Inland Empire, but they wanted to grow even larger. They started to chase yield, as in buying properties that might have been in challenging areas but had high cash flow, so to accomplish their goals they had to go out of town into areas that were more turbulent. They purchased apartment buildings in challenging parts of Texas and Arizona, and in order to afford buildings in each of those different markets, they went back and did what most people do: they refinanced to the max what they already owned.

They pulled money out by placing absolutely massive loans on the properties that they initially bought in Long Beach to fund the purchases in Riverside. Then they took out even larger loans on the Riverside buildings to pay for their purchases in Arizona. Then they borrowed from Arizona to pay for Texas and so on, but they drastically overleveraged.

As mentioned, refinancing is typically safe provided you're not overextending yourself. What this owner did was they took out massive loans, almost the equivalent of 100 percent of what the properties were worth at the top of the market. So the second the market took a hit in the recession of 2009, they were underwater. The net income of the buildings became drastically lower than the loan payments, and they previously spent all of their refinance proceeds on new purchases, so there was nothing left on reserve. All of their properties weren't performing, they quit making loan payments, and the bank foreclosed, and they lost everything. It's a sad story, but it's all too common.

If they hadn't placed such massive levels of debt on those properties, or if they just wouldn't have spent all of their cash refinance proceeds, they would have been able to survive the recession. But when the rents dropped and expenses went up, they just couldn't pay their bills. They had to give the properties back to the bank.

NO SUCH THING AS "RECESSION-PROOF"

"I'll buy at all ends of the economic cycle. If the price is right, I will buy. I feel that time is not important. It's the long-term value of the properties that is most important."

—PAUL LING

You can't avoid a recession. As we've discussed, the market is cyclical and self-correcting. More so, you can't plan for every possible scenario. At some point, you're going to be faced with a downturn and have to endure. It happens, but you shouldn't say, "I don't want to buy more buildings because I don't want to get hurt in a recession." Everyone from every walk of life gets hurt in recessions.

However, you can prepare for the worst and weather the bad times better than most. First, make sure you're not overleveraged, which means you don't have massive loans on your properties, typically no more than 60 percent of what the property is valued at. You can perform a stress test, as in run a model on your properties and see what happens if the rents drop 10 percent to 20 percent and also determine, if your vacancies go from 3 percent to 10 percent, with the loan you are thinking of putting on the property through a refinance, does it at least still break even? If it's completely upside down, maybe don't be so aggressive on loan amounts.

Second, always have some money saved. You need that rainy-day fund to help pay for the lean years. The bad times will come, but they will also pass, and typically massive opportunities lie on the other side.

It also helps to learn from the mistakes of others. Much of the time, the decisions that put owners in these tough predicaments seemed very sound at the time they made them. Hindsight, as we know, is 20/20. The owner that I previously discussed was wiped out; they started out purchasing buildings in Long Beach, and then when Long Beach became too expensive for them to be able to make any reasonable level of returns, they bought buildings in the Inland Empire of California, which was a more volatile market. A simple, sound strategy for them was, when Long Beach was too expensive they thought, "Where else can we get a decent return?" They went out to Arizona. Then Texas. The problem wasn't their plan, it was their execution and their timeline. By chasing yields as fast as they could refinance the last property, they made themselves vulnerable to a recession.

Now, casting a wide net is not a bad business strategy, but you need to keep it within your overall plan. When you're starting out, or even within the first decade of building out your portfolio, it's smart to buy buildings in an area with which you're familiar. You know the rental market and you have relationships with management companies, vendors, and maintenance people. It's when you go out of state and you have to rely on other people that you don't know as well to handle the properties that the troubles can occur.

The safe way is to continue in one area. If that foreclosed owner had just kept buying buildings in Long Beach, he would probably have been fine. If he had stayed diversified by acquiring buildings in Riverside, he probably would have been okay because the drive from where he lived to Riverside is only an hour. That means he only needed one property management company, one plumber, one HVAC technician, and he could quickly drive there to make decisions. When he started buying out of state, he doubled and tripled his overhead at the same time he entered into markets he didn't understand nearly as well.

WHY WOULD YOU BUY OUT OF TOWN?

"If it's an out-of-state property, I try to do some sort of co-op where my company manages rent collection and bill payment while the local firm deals with maintenance."

—RAND SPERRY

There are a number of reasons to explore real estate outside of your city. It could be that the market where you live is overheated. It could be that growth is flatlined because of overbuilding or employment. It could be the political climate is becoming a challenge. It could be that you discover opportunities outside of your hometown such as a city in a neighboring state opening a huge manufacturing facility and you want to get in before everyone else does and the prices rise.

With apartment buildings, sometimes you have regulations such as rent control that force you to deviate from your original plan. You thought it would be simple to purchase a building with low rents and raise everyone's rent from $1,000 to $1,200 a month and you either weren't aware of the local laws or all of a sudden the government passed new regulations and you simply can't raise rents at your discretion. Maybe you can raise them a few percent a year to keep up with inflation, but you're barely keeping up with your rising expenses.

I've worked with clients that have owned apartments in New York City, and it's been a complete nightmare for them. They recently passed laws and now they can't raise the rents at all and their expenses continue to rise. That's an economic catastrophe to find yourself in, especially for newer investors. Let's say you buy a building with an annual income of $100,000 with operating expenses of $40,000 and your loan payments are $45,000 annually, so you should still have around $15,000 of annual cash flow after all of your costs. In the next few years, your property taxes are going to increase as well as the costs of your insurance, utilities, and the labor to maintain and manage it.

Now your expenses went from $40,000 to $50,000. In the following year, the government gives you a minimal increase of a few percent and maybe you are now at $103,000, but your expenses went up again, now to $60,000 annually and your loan payments are still $45,000. It's now costing you $105,000 to operate a property with income of $103,000, which means your property is upside down and you are losing money. All this time, the value is plummeting because there's less net income, and the net income is what people buy when they are purchasing properties.

If you don't have the ability to control and increase the net income, you'll never be successful. If you buy in an area where that's out of your control, you're doomed to failure. It's critical that you do your due diligence including checking on the area's history of lease rate appreciation, job creation, and economic stability, and lastly, you need to feel positive about the political climate. If you feel that it's an area where there's a potential for operational issues with rent control or a place where rents never seem to rise in relation to expenses, you need to really think through how that can and will impact your investments.

Politics can change on a whim, and the market will always correct, but you can't fully prepare for natural disasters. Whether it's a hurricane, an earthquake or a global pandemic, disasters will strike and completely upend whatever plan you had brewing.

Natural disasters are exactly that, and you can't control them. All you can do is minimize your downside risk. You might not want to purchase a property that backs up to a forest, because if you're in wildfire country, you might have a fire and it's going to be hard to obtain insurance. You also might not want to purchase a property that sits next to a fault line or a floodplain, because if there's a huge earthquake or that proverbial one-hundred-year flood, your building could be utterly wiped out. At the very least, make sure that you can obtain reasonable insurance at a fair cost before you jump in on this purchase.

That doesn't mean you can't assume a little risk, but it means you need to research whether or not a disaster is likely, or just possible. It's okay to purchase a property close to an earthquake fault zone as long as you are factoring the risks and potential increased insurance costs. The property that you might want to avoid is the property that gets wiped out every ten years from a hurricane or tornado. Obtaining insurance loss runs will reveal the history of insurance claims and hopefully give you a fair idea of what you might expect.

I remember when I moved to California, my dad proclaimed, "There are earthquakes there all the time." Well, I've been here since '97, and there's never been an earthquake so bad that it caused anything or anybody any harm, but his beach house on the North Carolina Outer Banks has had dozens of hurricanes go through and cause numerous issues. If I had decided I didn't want to buy any real estate because I was worried about earthquakes, how far would I have gotten? You can't be worried about something that's out of your control. You simply need to factor in the risk.

David Soufer told me a while ago, "Brent, you're too worried about things that are outside of your control. You can't worry about politics, you can't worry about the economy. Make smart buying decisions based on what you've done in the past, because you're very conservative, and you're going to be just fine."

If you decide you need to explore greener pastures, that is a perfectly viable strategy. You just need to make sure you make prudent decisions.

BUYING OUT OF STATE

"I like to cluster buildings for asset management because that gives me economies of scale. I'll try to buy three or four buildings in one area, so I'm not having to take a long trip from one building to the next. Every day, I look at a sheet that has all my apartment buildings on it. There are about 42,000 units in those buildings. I rank each building according to a color code: red means there is some sort of problem, such as vacancies. Yellow means caution—we're starting to see vacancies or we're having trouble collecting rents."

—BOB HART

We have plenty of clients that have bought aggressively out of state but with low leverage. They didn't obtain a 90 percent loan at the purchase of a property in Arizona; they took out a 60 percent loan on that purchase. They also were very comfortable that they could raise the rents and survive a market correction. They felt comfortable because they spent the time upfront on the research, determining not only their upside but their downside risks.

They bought a building where the rents were $1,000 per month on average. By looking at comparable buildings, they felt confident that they could renovate and raise them to around $1,200. They also researched how far rents could fall, and they knew that even with a recession the rents shouldn't drop below $900.

Most people are hurt because they spend all their time trying to determine how much upside there is in a property, as in how much they can increase the income and improve the value of the property. They don't spend any time, or enough time, focusing on what the worst-case scenario could be in a down market.

If there's a recession, what could happen to the building? What could happen to the tenants? What could happen to the rents? If the rental rates drop, am I going to have enough net income to pay the bills?

People generally aren't skilled at underwriting or estimating their downside. That's where they get clobbered.

Plenty of people have started in California or New York and later bought buildings in Miami, Phoenix, Las Vegas, Chicago, Nashville, and Denver and they've done amazingly well for themselves. They have left their hometowns of Los Angeles, Chicago, or New York City and found a market that matched their business plan and had a mix of current cash flow and long-term rental growth. Most importantly, they bought with low leverage and they really had to dig in to understand those different areas, to understand how the building is going to operate in good times as well as the inevitable bad times.

If you've been buying apartment buildings in one particular area, and that area becomes so expensive that nothing makes sense, you really have three choices:

Choice number one, quit buying or just don't change your criteria and be comfortable with the fact that others will pay more and you won't land too many deals. Just wait patiently until there's a recession when you can buy buildings again after prices adjust. This philosophy tends to result in you never buying a building again, because you've effectively given up. As you can imagine, I don't hold by that strategy.

Choice number two is to just dig deeper, maybe going slightly outside the area you were buying in. If you were buying in an A neighborhood, maybe you now go to a B neighborhood or a C neighborhood. You dip slightly in quality to find a decent return but not head to such a rough area that you're going to have major issues. Maybe you go from buying retail with mostly credit tenants to purchasing well-located mom-and-pop stores.

Choice number three is head out of state. You leave San Francisco and buy buildings in Dallas.

Buying out of state, as we've discussed, comes with a number of caveats. You're going to need to be very confident in your ability to delegate. You'll need to research areas and select properties in an unfamiliar market. Most of all, you need to prepare to weather the financial storm should the market take a downturn. Your overhead increases dramatically when you expand your empire, so be sure to have enough money stored away for an emergency.

If those options don't sound in sync with your business plan, or the amount of effort you want to put forth, there is a fourth option: switch product types. If you've been buying apartment buildings, then you could switch to retail. For instance, right now, in the age of the internet, retail stores are getting clobbered and Amazon made their existence even more difficult. Office buildings aren't doing particularly well also. Big-box retailers, such as Toys-R-Us, Circuit City, and Borders, are going out of business and the stores sit vacant. Those vacant properties can often be purchased for land value, which is sometimes next to nothing.

THE STORY OF THE DEAL

"When I'm analyzing a property, I focus on gross rent multiplier, the cap rate, the price per square foot and the price per unit. I look to see if any of those factors are an outlier. Most buildings for sale are similar for these metrics, but if one of them is too high or too low in a negative way, I avoid it. However, if one of those four factors is really high or low in an attractive way, that signals to me that it could be a great deal and I try to buy that property. Now, when you go to sell you need to leave something on the table for the next guy who wants to buy the building. People will pay for upside in most markets."

—DANNY MONEMPOUR

The greatest value in real estate is often in buying *distressed* properties. Distressed means the building is not performing. It's either vacant, has a major operational problem, or the current owner just can't handle it. That's almost always the best opportunity provided you have a solution to the issue. But you have to ask yourself, "If it didn't work for the last guy, how's it going to work for me?" Everyone always thinks that they are smarter than the current owner, but are you?

As I mentioned before, there is always a story behind a property that is for sale. Some people believe that the story behind the deal is almost as important as the deal itself. For example, the story behind a property that was mismanaged and eventually foreclosed on. More often than not, a buyer will believe that if they purchase a property they can effectively manage it and make it work despite the prior owner's failures.

Maybe you see a property that's been owned for thirty years by the same individual. You might believe, "Well, there's an opportunity here because the person has owned it for so long and they might not be paying attention to where lease rates are today and it seems that they are renting their vacancies below market."

Flipping is exactly as I just described, buying and selling a property with fast renovations and rent increases to make a profit on the sale. A property that's been recently flipped is a type of property that savvy investors will avoid because they figure that the current owner has already repositioned it. The logic is that the current owner is most likely a sophisticated investor who bought the building on the cheap and is selling at a profit by repositioning it. What's the opportunity left for the next buyer? Remember, I said you need to leave some meat on the bone when you sell. By that same token, you need to look to purchase a building with some meat on it. Flipped properties often have little left for a new buyer to work with.

When buyers look and see a property owned by someone who also owns thousands of other units, they may think, "That's probably a sophisticated owner. What am I going to possibly be able to do to the property to improve it, to increase the value, to increase the rents, to lower the operating expenses, that the current owner didn't with all their resources, their experience, their time, and their money?"

PRICED TO PERFECTION

Don't always believe the financial information in the marketing materials presented to you by a seller or their listing agent. In most cases, these are idealized numbers—essentially portraying the property working under a perfect situation.

Almost everything on the market is what we call "priced to perfection." What that essentially means is that the seller and their broker, through the marketing materials, are showing how the property can cash flow if all the right conditions and operations are met.

The marketing materials might show the property at a 5 percent cap rate, but right now it's a 4 percent cap and the owner has priced the property to only be 5 percent under what they want you to believe are normal operating conditions. But it turns out, those are perfect operating conditions that you probably won't achieve: tenants paying above market rents (which is a higher lease rate than what is currently in place); lower expenses than realistic (most sellers and brokers use expenses much lower than reality in their marketing materials); and financing that may or may not be obtainable (leverage and interest rates).

Remember that the seller and the broker that they hire are trying to make the building look as attractive as possible to potential buyers, both on the physical appearance of the building as well as the appearance of the financial operations. So it's best to use caution and don't believe 100 percent of what is in a broker's marketing materials, as it probably describes an unrealistic situation of no vacancy, no repairs, an interest rate and high leverage loan that you will never get, and the tenant paying a higher lease rate than what the market will bear. Most properties advertised at a 5 percent cap rate, once you put realistic income and expenses in, are probably operating at closer to a 4.5 percent cap rate.

You can't always attempt to control the story when you're selling a property, but you always need to keep in mind how it affects potential buyers. A savvy broker will be able to handle some of those questions. In the end, you need to position the building as best you can, and then promptly move on to the next once you've taken it as far as you can.

ASSUMING A LITTLE RISK

"I do everything I can to avoid litigation. Litigation is about pain. When someone sues someone else, it's usually not about

*winning the lawsuit but about inflicting as much pain as pos-
sible so the other person caves and works out some sort of deal
with you."*

—FRED LEEDS

How will you know when you've taken too much of a risk? Unfortunately, the answer to that question might be when you wake up and you're facing a foreclosure or a lawsuit. You don't always know the risk that you take when the sun is up and shining. It's only when the sun goes down and we enter a recession or you are served with a lawsuit that you realize you made too many mistakes in what you purchased. However, as long as you have the staying power—and a rainy-day fund—you'll pull through.

The people that worry about being spread too thin are the people who often never grow their business. They're afraid of a recession, or of what happens when there's an earth-quake, or a fire, or when the economy dips and rents drop. Those are the people who are looking for excuses to never buy again.

So how can you assume a little risk and keep growing your portfolio? If you're buying with low leverage, and you have some funds left over for lean times, you should be able to survive any bad decision you make. Time heals all (or at least most) wounds when it comes to commercial real estate. Unless there's a major earthquake, or something that just wipes the building out completely, a rental market and the economy in a dense location will always come back. Always.

If you know that a downturn is inevitable, you can plan to endure a market drop. However, typically you never see it coming and you are caught at the worst possible moment. You've just bought a building and suddenly we enter a recession. What now?

There are always situations where somebody buys a shopping center, or they buy a giant building with a single tenant, and a year later, the tenant files bankruptcy. Now the owner has no income coming in and a huge expense on the building. That's a major problem, but as long as the person has funds left around to pay the mortgage, pay the property taxes, and pay for a leasing agent to go out and find them a new tenant, they're going to survive.

The one caveat is if you bought into a dying town. If you're buying in an area where the population's dwindling, and there's just no future, you're bound to lose out. You have to be very careful and buy buildings in an area where the population is growing, the economy is growing, and jobs are being created, because if not, what's the future going to be long-term? Increased population leads to increased rents, as long as there isn't a massive amount of new construction that's going to put thousands of new apartments or commercial space for lease on the market and create leasing competition.

This is why buying out of state shouldn't be done without planning. If you don't know the area or the market, you run the risk of purchasing a sinking ship. So how can you protect yourself from that scenario? How can you expand your empire in an intelligent way?

ROME WASN'T BUILT IN A DAY

"I have a vision for affordable and senior housing. My goal is to put people in quality housing that they couldn't afford elsewhere. City leaders enjoy working with me because of my track record and because I'm not greedy. As a result, I've been awarded contracts that I otherwise might not have gotten. Politicians know I'm honest, work hard, and take care of their constituents. When politicians from other cities see my work in neighboring cities, they want me to do projects in their city. They roll out the red carpet and assist me to find properties that need renovations and land to build in a short timeframe."

—THOMAS SAFRAN

If you want to expand your reach to an out-of-state market, you need to do your homework. The first thing you need is to find people you trust who have experience buying in those areas. Most people I know who have bought buildings out of state know *other* people who already performed well in those markets. A client of mine purchased several buildings in Denver, but they knew some other investors who had gone out there and bought retail, office buildings, and apartment buildings first with great success.

They had someone they could ask the preliminary questions, as well as some introductions to real estate professionals in that area: brokers and property management companies. They found somebody to show them around, to give them an understanding of what opportunities and pitfalls were in those areas. There might be a neighborhood that is quickly changing where you should be looking, but its reputation is so bad that you shouldn't buy there, at least not yet. A local can show you the real opportunities.

That is a huge challenge that people have to overcome when they're going into another area. Until you understand the market, you won't recognize the opportunities on your own. When you want to establish a foothold in areas you don't know, you need to buy with the least amount of risk. After you've bought that first building and become more comfortable, then maybe you can buy buildings in some more up-and-coming areas.

No matter what, you don't want your first building out of state to be a problem child. You don't want it to be a building that could be a maintenance nightmare, or in an area that's prone to problems, or that's going to underperform so much that it becomes a money pit.

It needs to be something that you can turn over to management and not have any trouble. Not to mention, if you have issues, it's not going to encourage you to buy more buildings in that area. That's a psychological roadblock you might never overcome.

I highly recommend that you start small. Don't decide, "I want to go to Salt Lake City and buy every apartment building," then drive out there and buy thirty buildings in one year. That's a recipe for disaster. You're spreading yourself too thin.

Once you've had a little success, and you have the capital to take larger risks, you can start playing the market, so to speak. You can start to diversify. Aim to buy more than one building at a time. Go into Salt Lake City and buy two apartment buildings, then go to Nashville and buy one building. Go to Reno and buy three. Perhaps you find out that Reno is going to open up a Tesla manufacturing facility—which they did—so there's going to be a ton of job creation, and rents are going to go gangbusters. You're sitting back thinking you're a genius because you bought three buildings there.

As with all risk, there is an upside and a downside. You could've gone into Atlanta and thought you were a genius by buying two buildings. Then all of a sudden Atlanta loses a massive amount of jobs, such as what happened to Detroit back in the day, and you're sitting there with vacant buildings. At least you only bought one or two buildings in that area. Diversification is huge, and if you're going out of state and into different cities, you probably don't want to put "too many eggs in one basket" until you're really, really comfortable with that area.

MONEY ON YOUR MIND

"I like to have the brokers I'm working with on a deal walk the property and give me feedback on it. I ask their advice on how to make the building look more presentable so I can get a better price for it."

—ABRAHAM STEIN

In a discussion some years ago, I was told that Europeans have a different mentality towards money. They don't mind having money sit in the bank. Americans, on the other hand, feel that it's a terrible thing to have cash sitting idle in the bank. They want to go out and spend it; they want to invest it. Paul Ling once told me, "The worst thing you can do is have money sitting in the bank doing nothing." Paul always seems to find great buildings to buy, so with good reason his cash doesn't sit idle for long.

I've known buyers that sweat when they have too much

sitting in the bank. "I could buy a property with this cash; why am I letting it just sit there?" I've also known the other side of the spectrum. "Ah, too risky right now. I don't want to do anything." People like that usually never buy another building. They've talked themselves out of the game.

For real estate investors, it's important to keep liquidity at the top of their mind. When they have money in the bank it's because of investments they made, sold, or refinanced, or because other investors trust them with their money, too. They want to invest, they want to try to grow their business. These are the people who are successful, provided they don't get over the tips of their skis. (I know, another old expression, but I use what works, as in the following story.)

A client of mine named Andre convinced his parents to give him some investment money and he purchased a building in a rapidly changing Los Angeles neighborhood. He had big plans for this investment, but he had to relocate the rent-controlled tenants, which meant he had to pay an exorbitant amount of money to get the building vacant by paying them to leave. Since he wanted his apartments to rent at an absolute premium, he spent a small fortune on extensive renovations.

Andre was already pushing his budget, so he didn't obtain permits for some of the work he wanted to do, such as installing laundry in all the apartments. He went vastly over budget with the goal of renting studio apartments for $2,000.

Meanwhile, at the end of the street, another client of mine developed a new Class A apartment building. Because he had 200 units, this owner decided he needed to fill his building up fast, so he offered a move-in special: $1,600 for studios in a flashy new building. This property was impressive to prospective tenants with a gym, jacuzzi, and all sorts of tenant amenities. Andre's small building was built in the 1950s and had no amenities like those, but he needed to obtain $2,000 for each studio apartment just to hit his numbers. Of course, he failed because somebody down the street built a flashy new building that totally undercut him.

He's been sitting on that property for two years with the building for sale and nobody wants to buy it at a price he can justify. It's worth about a half million dollars less than what he invested in it. Lesson learned: Be careful to not over improve.

You can't let obtaining high rents be the make-or-break decision of your business plan. Instead, you should consider taking a more "bread and butter" approach. More like the Holiday Inn: not fancy but not the cheapest. There will always be people who are looking for economical places to stay, whether overnight at a hotel or where they choose to live. As Keith Wasserman says, you need to run your own business like a Honda: practical and efficient.

If you buy a building with the assumption that you're going to obtain incredibly high rents and have your entire business plan revolve around that goal, you're setting yourself up for potential failure if you can't execute. Andre found this out the hard way. Not to mention the fact that when the economy changes, how will that affect rents in the area?

This is similar to those people we all know who have a steady, high-salary job and then buy a massive house. Well, what happens when they lose their job, or something else happens, and they don't have the money to make that huge monthly loan payment? All of a sudden they're underwater. They're bringing in $10,000 a month, and their mortgage is $15,000 a month. How are they going to pay that bill?

KEEP MOVING FORWARD

"I want my family to have a secure future. In ten years, I just want to be alive and healthy and watching the young people in my office take over and grow the business."

—RAND SPERRY

When you're first starting out, this process is slow. You're more involved with your properties, you're making all the decisions. As you delegate more and more responsibilities, you'll be free to focus on buying the next building. Whether that's in the same area, a different state, or even a different property type altogether, you need to keep moving forward.

It's also important to scale not just the amount of properties you own, but the size of those properties. While you may be comfortable with a few small four-unit buildings, the overhead and time-sink those create will eventually overwhelm you. You'll need to start to purchase larger properties.

There's a client of mine who owns one hundred duplexes. That's a hundred roofs, a hundred sewer lines, a hundred tax and utility bills, and a hundred nightmares waiting to happen.

There's another person I know who owns one apartment building that has 200 units in it. They have one roof to take care of and one sewer line. He and the other owner I mentioned both have 200 units, but the one has one hundred bills and the other one. Whose life is easier?

The point is that to scale your business, not only will you have to buy more and more properties, but you also need to try to purchase buildings that are larger and will require the same amount of work, but for considerably more units.

This isn't to say that you can't buy more buildings of the same size, but you need to think a few steps ahead. It's easy for you to manage ten properties with the help of a third party management company. Maybe when you own thirty buildings, you start building up your own team. But if you own hundreds of buildings in various locations in numerous states, the logistics are going to take up all of your time and energy. You won't have the mental capacity to look for a new deal to buy because you'll be spending twenty-five out of twenty-four hours a day just managing your chaos.

There's a fine line between being too aggressive and too conservative. At the end of the day, you have to walk that tightrope. You have to take calculated risks and manage your expectations on how much profit you're going to make. You have to pursue exponential growth, and at the same time think about how you'll handle a downturn in the economy.

You have to always remember that there will be bad times and you are going to need a plan to endure them.

My client Jeff found himself in a difficult situation. He bought a ton of real estate in the late '80s and early '90s, and then a recession hit in 1994. He lost almost everything. He was flat broke. But he didn't stop moving. That's about as big a setback as you can imagine and he managed to find a way to start buying buildings again a few years later. Now, he's a billionaire.

You will fail, and not every building you buy is going to be successful. That's a reality you have to accept when you're in real estate investments. No matter how careful you are, no matter how solid your business plan, there are going to be decisions you make that hurt you. The key is in knowing that those mistakes will happen, but never let that hold you back.

If you buy a hundred buildings, ten of them are not going to work out. They may underperform and maybe you'll need to sell at a loss or break even. The math generally goes like this: You buy a hundred buildings; thirty are going to be colossal home runs; sixty are going to do okay; ten will be dogs. If you sell the ten at a small loss, you have a tax write off for the ninety that you are doing so well on.

BUILDING AN EMPIRE

"How do you build an empire? One deal at a time. At first it was just me and my partner and my cousin and we ran the company out of my dad's house. Now we have asset managers, a project manager, and people to handle development. As we grew and needed more people, we hired them. Now, I am primarily focused on raising money, my strategic vision, and deciding what markets we want to be in."

—KEITH WASSERMAN

No matter how you divide and conquer the real estate world, the most important thing is to keep your momentum. You have to constantly be on the search for, or be actively purchasing, a new building. Additionally, as Andrew Tavakoli says, "You have to have the courage of conviction on when to buy and sell. You have to have the character of strength when everyone else is fearful and demoralized so you can keep your own council."

Shopping out of state is a viable option, but beware of the pitfalls. Seek out local advice, do your research, and start small so you can observe the new market. Don't be afraid to be aggressive, but understand that you will have setbacks along the way.

If you enter into a new asset class, the same advice applies. Research, find comparable buildings, and listen to people you trust who have gone this route before. If you're not comfortable exploring new assets, then focus on what you know. David Soufer says, "Good times or bad times, stick to what you're good at. Don't diverge your concentration."

If you look for a reason not to buy, you're done with investing. It won't be long before all you have left are excuses. Stay the course and keep moving forward. Jeff Elowe made his best investments while being a contrarian and having confidence to start buying when others were leaving. Right after the Northridge earthquake in 1994, Jeff became very aggressive while others told him, "You're insane buying apartments in Los Angeles."

Finally, and most importantly, don't spread yourself too thin. I remember learning that lesson from the Long Beach owner who lost everything. If you want to expand, and you should, make sure you research the areas and spread out in a controlled manner. Consult experts and listen to their advice. As your experience and confidence grows, so, too, will your portfolio.

CHAPTER 7

BUILDING TO
A BILLION

"During school, I worked as a property manager, earning extra cash by stocking the apartment building's soda vending machine and parking cars during football games at the nearby college stadium. After college, I worked for Pacific Life Insurance as an analyst.

"I went in with a friend and bought a seventy-year-old house in Santa Ana, Calif., for $60,000 and then spent weekends and evenings renovating the home. It was a learning experience. We invested $35,000 and sold the home for $130,000. Buoyed by our success, we bought four more houses in the next year. Me and my partner, David Kim, created a business plan in 1996, and that's when we quit our jobs and started buying and renovating properties."

—JERRY FINK

I had a client named Mr. Weiss, who is sadly no longer with us. Back in around 2002, I was walking into my office, and I saw him standing next to the elevator in the lobby. I was surprised to see him there, as I wasn't sure why he was in the office building. He had two giant paper bags, one in each hand, and they must have been two feet wide and two feet high.

I asked, "Mr. Weiss, what are you doing here?"

He smiled at me. "I'm here to see my accountant. I'm bringing him all the bills and receipts for all my buildings so he can put together the profit and loss statements."

This guy had two giant bags filled with papers covering everything he owned, which must have been thousands of bills and receipts. Mr. Weiss wasn't a real estate developer or some hotshot syndicator. He was a retired dentist. On the weekends, he used to drive around looking at apartment buildings to buy that were for sale. He was in his 80s at the point when we had this conversation, and he must have owned 200 properties. He'd started when he was in his 40s and just never stopped.

On his way back from his accountant, Mr. Weiss stopped by my office to see what I had for sale. I asked him, "Mr. Weiss, don't you have enough buildings? When is enough simply enough?"

He smiled at me. "Well, it's not that I need more buildings. My doctor told me that I need to keep busy, and I need to keep busy doing whatever gives me enjoyment in my life. And one of the only things that I really enjoy is buying apartment buildings."

I thought, "Wow, that's one of the most interesting answers I've ever heard anyone say about why they wanted to keep investing." But, whatever works. Whatever keeps you going. He lived about another ten years, and he passed away just recently, but in my mind I truly believe that the excitement of constantly working on the next deal to buy kept him alive for probably an additional decade beyond what would have been otherwise.

It's equally important to know that Mr. Weiss lived in a little house in a relatively modest Los Angeles neighborhood. This was a person who owned one of the largest collections of apartment buildings in the entire county of Los Angeles. He could have bought the biggest mansion in Beverly Hills or Hancock Park if he desired, but he didn't seem to have interest in that. For him, real estate wasn't about wealth or status; he just wanted to have fun buying apartment buildings. It was a hobby that kept him busy, and per his doctor, was keeping him alive.

You have to find your motivation. Are you in this for the

money? Are you in this for the status? Or is this just something that brings you joy?

When you're first starting out, the challenge is finding the money to buy the properties you want. As you progress further, the challenge will be finding the properties to buy that meet your criteria with all your available financial resources. It's no easy task, but the lessons are simple.

QUALITY, THEN QUANTITY

"Although in Mexico I had invested in some U.S. real estate deals—such as shopping centers—I didn't focus on real estate until I moved to Los Angeles in 1977. A friend from high school told me how to convert apartments to condominiums: You buy the property for $50 a square foot, invest $12 a square foot to fix it up, and then sell them for $100 a square foot as condos."

—ABRAHAM STEIN

The first thing to keep in mind is that you still want quality buildings. You can't lower your criteria just because you want to build a portfolio fast. There are a million stories about restaurant franchises that failed, and most are for one recurring reason: They opened up too many locations too quickly, and not all the locations performed as they estimated.

It's the same thing with real estate. You can't rush where

you're buying and how many deals you buy. It's great to have a goal of closing multiple transactions quickly, but you can't lower your criteria just to quickly accumulate properties. That's one of the quickest ways to fail. You have to maintain a standard.

No one fails by growing slowly. It's the people that take on too much too fast that suffer in a downturn. They're spread too thin, they're overleveraged, and they're vulnerable.

Once you have the machinery in place to quickly put together the funds that you need to acquire your next purchase that becomes your sole job. You should spend 90 percent of your day focused on how you're going to expand your portfolio. How are you going to buy more buildings, how are you going to find deals, where will they be located and the rest will fall into place? The property management company, the finances, those will be passing concerns that typically will all sort themselves out over time. You will have so many names in your rolodex that you will never be at a loss for assistance.

One of the things that separates the incredibly wealthy property owners from the people who own one or two buildings is experience. They know they can take the risk because they've done it so many times before. They're not jumping off a ledge hoping to land safely. They're safely walking down steps. Once you go through this process a few times, you already know what to do.

"Oh, the market's too hot. Things are just too expensive now. I want to wait until a recession or some other event makes prices drop to a level where I'm interested." That's just fear talking, and you only fear it because you don't have the experience or the foresight. Ask someone who is about to skydive for the first time versus their 100th time how fear changes with time, or more importantly, with additional experience. When you know what to expect and you trust the methods, you're not afraid to take the risk.

The ultimate goal some investors have is to have one or two groups put up *all* the money, as opposed to dozens of small investors. We've worked with multiple investors who are backed by a single pension fund or some other single source of capital and it's much easier for them to operate as they often only have one group to report back to, making the investor relationship job much simpler on a daily basis. This investor or group will put up all the capital required on a given transaction, and then you as the sponsor are enabled to locate and purchase properties that meet the criteria of you and your investors. With those resources, you can expand rapidly and develop a dense portfolio.

As you expand, you have to manage your growing financial liabilities as well.

AN INTERESTING PRINCIPAL

When you're first starting out, it's a struggle to put together the cash necessary for the down payment on your first investment. It's a challenge to keep finding sources of equity to buy the properties that you find. After a while, you have a new problem, which is you have enough equity to purchase just about whatever you can find, but it's a struggle to find the properties you want. Between those moments, you'll likely uncover an issue with your loan payments.

When you take out a loan, your lender will apply an interest rate based on a number of factors, from market conditions to your credit and experience to assets you own to the balance of your checking account. As you start paying off that loan, your monthly loan payment covers both the interest and the principal, or the full value of the loan.

Let's just say you have a 5 percent interest rate with your lender. If you have a $1 million dollar loan on a property, your annual payments in interest equate to $50,000 a year, which is a little bit over $4,000 a month. On top of that, if you have an amortizing loan, you're paying each month towards principal reduction, which could be another 50 percent above what you are paying monthly in interest. Once you're up to twenty to thirty buildings, you could have a massive amount of principal reduction happening every month. Now, this isn't great for cash flow as well as your taxes, which is why so many investors, including myself, favor interest-only loans.

At this point, you have two things going in your favor. One, you own these properties, you're improving them, and you're systematically raising the rents, which then effectively raises the value of the building. You're adding equity to the property by adding value through rent increases. The second thing you're doing passively is just making loan payments, which is paying down the principal (assuming you have an amortizing loan).

After a while, you're self-funding all of your own purchases through the equity that you're refinancing out of your own buildings. That is one way to keep growing this empire.

The second way is with an influx of capital through investors. As you grow more successful, all of your friends, family, business colleagues, and other professionals in the industry are going to notice what you're doing. The next thing you know, you will have others willing to give you substantial amounts of capital for your upcoming deals. The success you have is going to draw others to you, like bees to honey, and those bees are bringing capital with them, but it can sting you if you aren't careful, and sometimes even when you are.

When you're using your own money and equity to fund

purchases, you're limited by your personal assets and your own capacity for risk. As you add investors, you not only increase your available funds to purchase larger buildings, you spread that risk out. While that can sometimes be a negative, most often you find that large groups are able to weather risk at a greater scale. Being a part of a group also allows you to purchase larger properties sooner than you would have alone.

Jeff Elowe owns a national real estate corporation called Laramar Group. Jeff and a partner started buying small apartment buildings in Chicago and Miami in the late 1980s. When the markets that they were focused on at the time became overheated, they pivoted to Los Angeles and kept their momentum as they continued expanding.

At this stage, money is no longer the limiting factor in your portfolio. It's your willingness to put in the energy and keep your momentum going. If you want to reach the top tier of this industry, you should take a note from the most successful members. Stop looking at it as a job and start thinking of it as a game.

PLAYING THE GAME

"I love the intellectual challenges of investing in real estate. I enjoy the process and I relish the challenge of trying to do better."

—JEFF ELOWE

There is a common thread I've seen when people make the pivot of owning several buildings to owning dozens of buildings: it becomes a game. It's like Monopoly. The goal is gathering up as much property as possible provided that it meets your criteria, and you're always thinking a few moves ahead.

It becomes easy, because you're unburdened from the minutiae of dealing with the property once you own it. It's a game and here are the steps broken down:

- You find a property to purchase that meets your criteria.
- You put a transaction together—offer, counter offer, opening escrow, etc.
- You develop a business plan about how you're going to operate the property.
- You obtain a loan and close the escrow.
- You turn it over to management, and maybe once or twice a week you'll speak with them about each property.
- You continue the search for the next building.

Your goal of adding to your portfolio will simply be broken down into something this simple! Your primary focus is buying more buildings and then having management execute on your business plans.

Your second focus is how to finance the next property

through either investors or your own resources. There are a million people and organizations all desiring to invest in a great real estate deal. You need to demonstrate to them that you can operate the property and be a reliable sponsor. That is what separates the successful investors from the rest: whether or not they can find deals to buy.

The game is drastically simpler when you're using your own equity to fund purchases. The decisions you make, and the consequences, all fall right on to you. When you start to explore investor groups, the rules change. You have to consider the positions of everyone contributing to the purchase.

Huge corporations don't have much threshold for risk. If there is a potential for litigation, tenant-related issues, questionable neighborhood, or local political climate risk, they probably won't invest in it. Corporations don't typically want to purchase rent-controlled or rent-stabilized buildings because they don't want to deal with regulations limiting their ability to execute on their business plan.

If I buy a property on my own and it doesn't work out well, I can blame myself and it's clearly my problem to deal with. If I take someone else's money and buy a property, and it doesn't work out well, they're blaming me. Now, I'm in trouble with not only my personal money but also with my investors' money. The level of risk just goes up drastically. You can only blame so much on the market and you can only blame so much on timing. At the end of the day, your investors are going to point the finger at you, and you're going to have to explain why the investment either failed or didn't live up to their expectations.

PLAYING WITH OTHER PEOPLES' MONEY

"I tend to avoid getting into partnerships with people who are wealthier than me. They have different goals. Sometimes, they want assets and sometimes they just want to buy property. Sometimes, they want cash flow. This creates challenges because your partner's aims could be much different from yours."

—DAVID POURBABA

Taking other people's money and investing it for them has a number of pros and cons. When you're first building your portfolio, it can be very helpful to have the extra support and capital. You can do more to add value if you have more money available. Later in your career, as your equity grows, you can be more selective about using other peoples' capital versus your own. Maybe you enjoy the dynamic you've created with a particular investment group, or maybe you want to venture out on your own. Once you become more established, you'll have those options.

Several clients of mine who have specialized in real estate syndications, when they initially offered their first investment deals, would allow people to invest with a minimum contribution between $10,000-$20,000. They ended up with individuals who wouldn't be what you would typically consider "qualified investors," providing equity in small amounts. It might be necessary to use small tranches from multiple investors on your first deals, as you probably won't have a choice, but there are drawbacks.

What happens is those investors almost always become a pain in the neck. Even though they've only invested a small amount, they're the ones constantly calling and asking you about cash flow, renovations, and when the property will be sold. Large investors tend to understand the business and tend to just read over the reports provided things are going as planned.

The first two to three deals, you can't be as picky about your investors because you're happy to just have people to put money in. Over time, once people see how well you're doing, you will start to move up the minimum investment. On your next purchase, you will alert your prospective investors that you aren't taking a minimum of $10,000 anymore by stating, " A minimum of $50,000, or a minimum of $100,000, is required to invest in this property."

You'll end up with fewer investors in every deal, but the investors are going to be willing to put up more equity. It's going to work out better for you in the long run with more professional investors.

I invested in a hotel in El Segundo several years back. The sponsor's original goals were to keep the minimum investment at $100,000 or more; however, the real estate broker who sold him the property and her boyfriend both wanted in on the deal. Neither were wealthy and he let each of them invest a small amount, which turned out to be a massive mistake. The boyfriend needed this money to support his lifestyle and didn't understand that the business plan was to fully renovate the property and that there wasn't going to be any immediate cash flow. While he only had maybe 1 percent of the equity in the property, he caused 90 percent of the investor headaches and now all of us were stuck with him.

Once you've proven yourself as a sound operator, the dollar amounts tend to jump dramatically. The investors might be willing to give you $5 million or $10 million and just drop it into an account. Sometimes, you'll have to start making interest payments to them immediately. That's a very daunting task, because if you don't quickly use the funds to make purchases, you'll have to pay interest on money that you haven't spent, with no new cash flow.

An approach that most sponsors take is to set up discretionary funds. When they find something to purchase, they approach their investors and alert them, "I need you to fund $2 million for this deal." The investor reviews the prospectus, and if they approve it, they send in the money.

Donald Sterling, the previous owner of the Los Angeles Clippers and one of the largest apartment owners in Los Angeles, reportedly did something similar around 2005. Allegedly, a bank provided him a line of credit for around $50 million. He had to start paying interest on the funds the second they gave it to him. If it was 3 percent annually, he was making payments equivalent of around $120,000 a month. He had the daunting task of having to quickly find $50 million worth of apartment buildings to purchase to put the money to work.

He bought everything that he felt would work for him in Los Angeles, acquiring buildings in transitioning neighborhoods that he typically wouldn't have bought. He had this tranche of money and the pressure of needing to allocate it. He knew that if he didn't spend the money, he was paying interest on it regardless. In Donald's case, his aggressive tactics worked, and now he looks like a genius having invested in areas that he previously skipped over. The bank's investment in him allowed him to take on a huge amount of property and considerably grow his real estate empire.

Not too many people are going to find themselves in that situation, having that kind of equity arriving all at once. Often, it's in a fund and you can start drawing from it as you need. You let the investors know the details and ensure they know the projected rate of return.

Whether you choose to work alone or with investors is up to you. Everybody finds their comfort level and develops a long term plan and continues to push in that direction. As you find more and more success, the pack around you starts to change. Your investors are no longer millionaires but rather some of the wealthiest people in the world. With that wealth comes a new mentality.

THE THREE COMMA MENTALITY

"You have to love the game. You must have a drive to do good while you're doing well. You must have a drive to be relevant. If you're doing good things for people, that keeps you wanting to do more. I'm trying to create a better wheel, not a new one."

—BOB HART

There was a client of mine, maybe ten years ago, who wanted to buy a particular building. The seller asked me, "I need to see his proof of funds so that we can make sure that he has enough money for the down payment to buy the property." That's a very common request, as sellers want to make sure you can afford the purchase. I asked the very humble buyer to provide proof of his financial situation. He said, "No problem, I'll send it to you." A few hours later, he sent me his statement for his stock portfolio at Charles Schwab.

I saw the number and stopped in my tracks. I counted the

zeroes. Then I counted the commas. It was more than $100 million, and he had just nonchalantly emailed it to me.

It made me think, "This guy has $100 million in Charles Schwab. How much money does he have in all the apartment buildings and office buildings and shopping centers he owns?" It was really a revelation because he was a simple apartment building owner. His *backup* investment was his Charles Schwab account.

When you're interacting with somebody who has that kind of portfolio, it changes your relationship. Those people don't always want my advice. They've gotten very far in life doing things their way. They might want my opinion, but they're not necessarily going to follow it.

When you're a billionaire, your outlook is radically different. You don't worry about the small details of managing a property. You're not worried about where the finances will come from, or whether or not you can handle the risk. You're looking for one thing: access to investments.

Over the years, I've worked with several billionaire investors. I'm convinced that the only reason they even take calls is because they're hoping some random person is calling them with an amazing deal for them to buy. They wake up in the morning and the one thing that they want to do is find the next deal. It's a game for them. It's a chase.

Some people, like my father, wake up early on a cold November morning to go hunting for deer. Some people go trout fishing. Then there exists a small segment of our population that wakes up in the morning looking for the next building to acquire. That's the single thing that drives them.

These are Type A, self-starter, self-motivated, entrepreneurial individuals who have close to everything figured out. For some, their entire day revolves around creating new streams of wealth and no other aspects of their life are of much importance. Still, there are billionaires who have very well-rounded lives. They take long vacations. They spend time with friends and family. They've figured it out.

That is your competition. You have to ask yourself, are you ready to stand shoulder to shoulder against them?

When I was just starting out, I was willing to work fourteen hours a day and constantly be on the phone trying to set up appointments. I was desperate to succeed, and with no family or distractions and endless bills to pay, I had nothing else to do. On the first properties I bought, I didn't exactly have massive amounts of capital sitting in the bank. I just knew, "These are good deals. I need to figure out a way to buy them." I did whatever I could to put the purchases together, and I was confident in myself that I'd be able to make it work.

Eventually, you'll reach a point where you'll ask, "Do I have enough properties? Should I take more chances?" The people that become billionaires never feel they have enough. They always want more. They never take their foot off the gas. They're always full throttle trying to find the next deal, making investments that are just as risky as the ones they made when they were younger. Sometimes, that level of risk-taking makes people billionaires. Other times, of course, it can bring them to bankruptcy.

People usually start out being very conservative in this business. Once they become wealthy, their ego gets so large that they often become less conservative. They think, "I'll make it work because I'm smarter than everyone else." Those people often get hurt, but it's rarely a permanent setback. They might buy ten properties and two don't work out well. The next challenge is to keep the two that don't work out from wrecking the eight that are healthy.

The point is everyone's criteria will be different. Everyone's appetite, everyone's will, and everyone's capacity for risk is unique to them. If you want to stick it out and build that billion dollar portfolio, you need to identify your level of risk.

FINDING YOUR LEVEL OF RISK

"I started to slow down after a bad automobile accident several years ago. I now buy for my children and for fun. Going into

the office is a force of habit, but I only work about three or four hours most days and spend the rest of my time enjoying life."

—DAVID SOUFER

In this industry, there are three tiers of investors: The first is people who own one or two apartment buildings. For whatever reason, they never pursued it further. Then there are people who own around ten buildings. Finally, there are the people who own a hundred or more buildings. Interestingly enough, there are very few people who own forty or fifty or sixty. They either own a couple, a dozen, or a hundred.

People typically start out buying at the bottom of a market or as it runs up, and they purchase one or two investment properties. They're fairly conservative at first because they're coming out of a recession and their appetite for risk is very low. They buy one building, they buy a second, and maybe they pick up a third. After five years, they own ten buildings, and at that point we're probably at or just about at the top of the real estate market. Cracks start to appear in the investment world and they are nervous.

What happens is that they can go in two different directions. They could say, "We seem to be at the top of the market, the deals don't make sense anymore, and I'm just going to be conservative and wait it out." Those people often never buy buildings again. Reminiscing of the "good old days," the deals will never be good enough for them and they're always going to find a reason not to buy. They've officially taken their foot off the gas.

The other type of investor says, "You know what? I'm going to keep buying, but it feels overheated so we need a new business plan. Maybe I'll go out of state. Maybe I'll buy a different asset class, such as industrial properties." Some of these people will fail, but most will find success and never stop buying buildings.

At the end of the day, they typically come out drastically farther ahead because they continued to invest throughout the entire cycle of the market. You never know when you're at the top. You never know when you're at the bottom. You just have to keep buying, keep finding deals that work for you, keep growing. In any market, there's always opportunities. You can find incredible deals if you have the right criteria and the right business plan.

THE HOTTEST CLUB

"If I wake up in the morning, I'm going to look for a building that I don't own. I still pick up the phone and cold-call every day. I call owners to see if they'll sell me their buildings."

—FRED LEEDS

Finding deals to purchase is the hard part. When you find deals and you've become an established investor, the equity oftentimes comes to you. In some ways, it's like running a club. A friend of mine was in the nightclub business and told me, "The way to make a nightclub successful is to find a way to attract either celebrities or really attractive people in the door. You become friends with people who run modeling agencies. Maybe you take the models out for dinner or a big night out on the town and then afterwards you take them over to your new club. People will then tell their friends about how much fun they had and about how incredible the place is. The next thing you know, there's a line out the door to get in."

Real estate works the same way. If you buy a few properties and quickly sell them for massive profits and people find out, investors will express interest in working with you. It becomes easier once you've established this track record, but to do that, you have to make yourself the hot new nightclub in town. You have to demonstrate that you have the expertise in turning deals around for a huge profit. You have to create a compelling story.

I recently received an email from Keith Wasserman, who is one of the owners of Gelt, Inc. The company periodically sends out press releases to announce their latest success story, such as, "Gelt, Inc. sells 400-unit apartment property for $92 million after a three-year hold in Lakewood, Colorado." It readily lists who the real estate brokers were. They put comments in about what they've accomplished and who they are. They've created the story for future investors and shown how they've made an enormous profit for their clients. It's a compelling story and establishes credibility through hard facts.

They also send out emails about Gelt-exclusive investment offerings: "Dear Investor, Gelt is excited to present our next exclusive investment opportunity. We are acquiring a 390-unit apartment community in Denver, Colorado, with tremendous value add upside. Conservatively, the project is expected to produce an estimated cash return on 8.22 percent to the investors over a likely anticipated hold period with an estimated investor equity multiple of 2.2X."

If you're just starting out, or just closed on your tenth property, how can you put your story in front of investors? It might be easier than you thought. The media loves interviewing investors about something that's relevant to their subscribers. If it's a real estate publication, they are always looking for interesting and relevant stories to run. If you can give them a compelling story about how you bought an apartment building for $5 million and two years later sold it for $8 million, they'd love to publish that.

There are hundreds of online portals that offer these real estate services and stories. They're national websites, and you just have to reach out to them and provide them the details on your successful transaction. If your deal story is fantastic with relevant content they will publish it, and the next thing you know, they and others are calling you looking to see what next deal you are working on.

You're selling yourself as an expert, and it's one of the most important sales of your career.

Everything in life is sales. You're constantly selling yourself. When you tell these success stories about how you bought an apartment building for $20 million and sold it three years later for $30 million, you're just highlighting the best things that have happened. You're editing out the less important details of the transaction.

You're probably not going to highlight how challenging it was to manage the property: the roof problem you had in the rain storm; the gang problem in the neighborhood; the fact that you had twenty vacant units and couldn't find tenants; the contractors who ripped you off or the ones you had challenges paying because you didn't have any cash flow during renovations.

You're not necessarily hiding those facts, but you certainly aren't showcasing the less-than-memorable parts of the story. Instead, you sell yourself with only the great aspects of the deal. It's sales. Life is all about sales, and this business is no different.

TREASURE HUNTING

"For me, it's not about making money. I like the intellectual challenge. I like being engaged and being productive and playing the game well. Insecurity is a great motivator. I try to stay focused on my legacy and my significance."

—ANDREW TAVAKOLI

Abraham Stein was born in Mexico City, and after immigrating to the United States started buying properties in West Hollywood with a business partner and, as previously mentioned, converting them to condos, which they sold individually for a profit. Then, they moved into buying apartment buildings as long-term investments and doing the same. Abe's success allowed him to do what he wanted, which was to spend most of his life traveling and with his large family.

He'd go on vacation for three weeks, then he'd come back for two and then head out on a new exotic adventure. He was constantly coming and going. You'd call his cell number and get an out-of-the-country signal and you knew he was somewhere else.

I sat down with him once and he told me, "Look, I like buying buildings because I love the action of trying to find the next deal. The thrill of the chase. Trying to find the next property."

Reza Etedali, a real estate broker who I once worked with, told me back around 2000 that he looked at prospecting—which in brokerage is cold-calling owners—as treasure hunting. It would take hundreds of calls to strike gold, which was an owner saying, "Hey, I'm ready to sell my 50,000-square-foot shopping center in Irvine." If you didn't make the call to the guy, and get him on the phone at that particular moment, he would never have told you that. Some other broker would have made the call and been awarded the business.

This entire business is often simply reduced to who is the best at treasure hunting. Reza could find a treasure by picking up the phone and calling property owners, and plenty of investors do the same thing. They're calling brokers saying, "Hey, what have you got for sale? What's coming up?" They're out looking. They are being proactive about finding the next property, not waiting for a flyer to show up in the mail.

After a while, you've established the criteria for what you'll purchase. On your first few deals, you spend hours just sitting there trying to figure out if it will work with a variety of homemade Excel spreadsheets, making all sorts of estimations on what annual repairs are going to run, what rent growth projections you hope for, and what's going to happen with interest rates in five years when you need to refinance or sell the property. You're making all these assumptions about where the financial world is going to be in the future, and it never works out as anyone predicts. Who could have predicted 9-11, the subprime collapse, or COVID-19?

Once you've bought five, ten, or fifteen of these buildings, you understand how things generally work. You just plug the financials into a model and say, "Yes, this appears to work. I'll buy it." You've gone through this process so many times that you can very easily look at a property and know whether it's going to work or not.

As a real estate broker, I'm selling people buildings and typically representing the seller, and 90 percent of those buildings I don't necessarily think are great deals on the surface. Everything has value at the right price, for sure. A piece of land in the middle of nowhere only has value if you can sell it to somebody else for a profit or maybe, despite it being in the middle of nowhere, you can build something on it that justifies your purchase. But if you don't have a business plan, not even a bargain is worth the money.

There's a building I just sold in the Los Angeles area and I thought it was terribly overpriced. Six months later, I asked the new owner, "How's the building coming along?"

To my surprise he said, "Great. I converted all the two-bedrooms into three-bedrooms and dramatically raised the rents. I turned the basement into an office and rented it out. We're renting some of the apartments furnished and we're able to charge twice the rent that the previous owner was getting."

I looked at him and thought to myself, "Wow, I never would have thought of that." All I'd seen was a very marginal deal, but he saw a hidden treasure and found the gold.

A BIGGER PORTFOLIO, THE SAME MISSION

"I love this work. It excites me. I might slow down if the excitement fades, but for now I love the feeling of knowing, 'I won.' I get a rush from buying buildings. I get a sense of success and accomplishment when I close escrow on something."

—DANNY MONEMPOUR

Once you understand the basics of this business, it's just about consistency. You need to keep moving, keep your momentum, and take calculated risks. That's really all there is to it. People at the top of this industry stay aggressive no matter where the market might be. They simply adjust their criteria to adapt with market conditions.

Adjusting your criteria is the key to long-term survival in real estate. If it's the top of the market, you can keep buying—you just have to remember to stay focused on maintaining your standards. You have to be regimented and you can't just buy because you want to spend money. You can't be like a five-year-old who gets his allowance and runs straight down to the candy store. You have to save capital for a rainy day. Don't just look at the upside; keep the worst case in mind, too.

If the market collapses, what happens to my rents? If the rents drop 10 percent, am I going to still be able to pay the bills and hang on? People fail because they have so much money behind them during good times that they're not focused on what happens in the bad times. They have investor money and they think that protects them from being wiped out.

They're not thinking about the risk as much because it's not always their own money. However, they have a fiduciary requirement to look out for their investor's best interests.

Resist the temptation to take bigger, unnecessary risks when you have investor money burning a hole in your pocket. You do need to pursue your next purchase with a sense of urgency, but don't let that cloud your judgment. Be smart and move forward with purpose.

CONCLUSION

THE HARD WORK AHEAD

"You have to anticipate problems and deal with them before they become worse. A good offense is your best defense. Many property owners are too focused on expansion, and that's a real problem when you're not paying attention to your operations. The buildings develop problems that could have been avoided if they'd paid more attention to them."

—BOB HART

In January 2020, COVID-19 made its first appearance in the United States. In just a few months, its virulent nature led to global shutdowns and entire populations required to stay in their homes for months. The world economy took a major hit, and with it, the real estate industry suffered a major blow.

In July of 2020, after the United States previously had an

unprecedented unemployment rate of around 3 percent, businesses shut down and approximately 20 percent of the country was unemployed almost overnight. The gross domestic product tumbled 33 percent in the March to June 2020 period, the worst in recorded history. Nobody ever thought this could happen, and commercial properties—from office buildings to retail centers to apartment buildings—all suffered from tenants not paying rent.

If you're reading this in 2021 or 2022, you're living through history. It's a challenge that we as a species haven't faced since the Influenza Pandemic of 1918. Thankfully, we have come out on the other side.

However, you cannot deny that this was a financial disaster for many people. With job closures and non-essential businesses shutting down, millions lost their jobs. A loss of jobs and business closures meant that landlords were burning money at both ends.

When I caution that you need to have money on reserve for an emergency, this is the most extreme version. You have to be able to survive the worst-case scenario.

During disasters, it's easy to lose focus on what's important. Understand that money can be made again. Lost income can be found. The people around you—your family, your friends, your neighbors—they are what really matter. When you're knocked down, know that you are able to make it through together.

And when you pick yourself up, reach down to help the next person.

HEAL, REBUILD, THRIVE

"You can never have enough. I love what I do. I love making money. I love making my friends money. And this business is a safe way to make and preserve wealth."

—KEITH WASSERMAN

I've learned over more than twenty years that this business is filled with highs and lows. Coming out of the recession in 2010, I saw opportunities all around me. Now, staring at the valley during the 2020 pandemic, I know that those same opportunities will come again.

Building the billion dollar portfolio is not easy. It takes incredible will, hard work, and the ability to weather a few storms. Once you understand the formula, it's not so hard to understand.

First, you need to identify the type of property you want to buy. Do your research, ask around, and be confident in your decision. My advice, which you read previously, is to always look for a heavily devalued property.

Once you know what you want to buy, you need to come up with the money. Use the assets and equity you have or partner up with investors and make an informed decision on how to proceed. Most of all, make sure this is performed with a long-term plan in mind.

Now that you have the property, add value with intelligent renovations. Don't waste money on expensive mechanical or cosmetic repairs and upgrades that won't bring you increases in rent. If you choose to make cosmetic updates, think about what makes sense from a buyer's perspective.

When you go to list the property for sale, find a broker who you are comfortable working with. Listen to their advice. They make their money by taking their clients' properties and positioning them to sell. They'll know what to do.

During all of this, never stop looking for the next property to buy. If you follow these steps and never lose focus, you can build a billion dollar portfolio.

Real estate investing is an incredibly lucrative business, and it can and should be enjoyable as well. While no casual stroll in the park, it doesn't require anything more than your time and energy to be successful. If your goal is to reach the pinnacle of this industry, I believe I've laid out a clear path. If you have any questions, I am always happy to help.

Brent Sprenkle

310-621-8221

Sprenkleapartments@gmail.com

Now that you have the tools, the only question is: What do you want to buy today?

SPECIAL THANKS

This book encapsulates hundreds of collective years of real estate experience. While I'm confident in my approaches, I wouldn't have been able to put this all together without the help of some incredible people.

PAUL LING

Born in Malaysia and educated in Australia, Paul moved to the United States after college and started his career as an auditor. After purchasing a few small apartment buildings, he caught the real estate bug and eventually quit his job and is now one of the largest private owners of smaller class A apartment buildings in West Los Angeles.

DAVID POURBABA

David Pourbaba is CEO and founder of 4D and Development Investments. Born in Iran and educated in England before moving to the United States, David's original career was as an engineer designing drive-through windows for McDonalds. He and some friends hit it big importing furniture from China, assembling it in their spare time, and selling it to stores. Soon afterwards, they bought their first property and real estate investment exploded afterwards. Now, David is one of the largest owners and developers of apartment buildings and commercial properties in Los Angeles and Las Vegas.

DAVID SOUFER

Born in Iran, David started to manage commercial properties while in college at UCLA. While planning on going to medical school, he ended up going into commercial real estate full time as the management business led him to purchasing properties with his clients. Afterwards, he realized that he had the management expertise to purchase distressed properties in Los Angeles and is now the largest owner of apartment buildings in the Mid-Wilshire area of Los Angeles. In addition, David has one of the largest collections of rare Ferraris in the world.

JERRY FINK

Jerome A. Fink is a co-founder and Managing Partner of The Bascom Group, LLC. Bascom has completed over $15 billion in multi-family and commercial value-added transactions since 1996, including more than 600 multifamily properties and 160,000 units. Bascom has ranked among the top fifty multifamily owners in the U.S. Bascom's subsidiaries and joint ventures include the Southern California Industrial Fund, Rushmore Properties, Bascom Portfolio Advisors, Shubin Nadal Associates, Spirit Bascom Ventures, REDA Bascom Ventures, MHF RM Holdings, Bascom Northwest Ventures, Bascom Arizona Ventures, Harbor Associates, Village Partner Ventures, and the Realm Group. Bascom's subsidiaries also include Premier Business Centers, the largest privately held executive suite company in the U.S.

ABRAHAM STEIN

President of Kmm Management, Abe started his career as the largest producer of rebar steel in Mexico. After moving to the United States, he and a friend started to convert apartment buildings into condominiums and then he began to purchase apartment buildings. Abe is now one of the largest private party owners of mid-sized apartment buildings in the Koreatown and Hollywood areas of Los Angeles.

RAO YALAMANCHILI

The principal at PI Properties, Rao was born in India and moved to the United States to pursue a masters degree in engineering. He settled in Los Angeles and began working for an air quality board. After finding out that the onsite manager at the apartment building he lived at received free rent with little work required, he moved into another apartment building as the manager. A colleague at work purchased a small apartment building and Rao then realized that he could do it, too. His maintenance and management experience made him a unique buyer, and he eventually found an owner willing to sell to him and provide the financing for his first purchase. Rao is now one of the largest private owners of non-institutional quality apartment buildings in Los Angeles.

DANNY MONEMPOUR

Danny took a real estate course in college and was intrigued. Shortly afterwards, after 9/11, he found a willing seller and managed to purchase his first building with almost no down payment. Afterwards, he became one of the most active buyers of apartment buildings in Los Angeles County, founding Monem Corporation in 2002. Since its inception, Monem has successfully onboarded more than 120 acquisitions throughout the greater Los Angeles area from diverse client backgrounds.

RAND SPERRY

Rand Sperry had been a well-known real estate and business leader in Southern California for nearly thirty-five years. In 1987, Mr. Sperry was the co-founder of Sperry Van Ness. Under his leadership, the organization he co-founded grew into a national real estate brokerage firm. Mr. Sperry is also a co-founder of Sperry Commercial, Inc. and Sperry Equities, LLC.

FRED LEEDS

Mr. Leeds is responsible for the overall strategic direction of Fred Leeds Properties and its real estate operation. He is responsible for directing the investment activities of the company, including acquisitions, development, value-added projects, and dispositions. Fred attended the University of Southern California. His active participation in the community has earned him several awards and accommodations including the City of Los Angeles Mayor Certificate of Appreciation Award for the Improvement of the Model Neighborhood Program Target Area.

KEITH WASSERMAN

Keith Wasserman founded Gelt, Inc. in 2008 during the height of the recession and financial meltdown. Keith has been involved in the acquisition of several commercial, industrial, and residential properties, mainly in the Western U.S., now totaling over $1.5 billion in assets. As co-founder of Happy Home Communities in 2017, Keith added the manufactured home venue to the growing list of entrepreneurial ventures he's involved in. He oversees the company's operations, marketing, investor relations, acquisitions, leasing, development, and disposition services. Keith graduated in 2007 from the University of Southern California from the Marshall School of Business. Keith leads Gelt's charitable giving program and recently teamed up with Damian Langere to form The Resident Relief Foundation, a 501(c)(3) public non-profit whose focus is on helping renters avoid eviction upon an unexpected financial emergency. Keith is also a member of YPO (Young Presidents Organization).

ANDREW TAVAKOLI

Beginning in 1987, Andrew Tavakoli started investing, renovating, managing, and leasing apartment buildings through syndication. Over the past thirty-three years, Mr. Tavakoli has invested and transacted over $1 billion of primarily retail and apartment projects nationwide through the umbrella of Tavaco Properties, LLC. Mr. Tavakoli has extensive experience acquiring REO and non-performing loans directly from Financial institutions, including banks and special servicers.

THOMAS SAFRAN

Thomas Safran is Chairman of Thomas Safran & Associates, developers and managers of affordable multifamily residential housing. His firm specializes in both family and senior low-rent housing and mixed-use developments. Nationally, Mr. Safran has belonged to such organizations as the Home Builders; the Urban Land Institute; the National Housing Coalition; NAHRO; and the National Leased Housing Association, of which he was a member of the Board of Directors. He has been active locally in Los Angeles nonprofit housing organizations as President of Alternative Living for the Aging, Vice President of Menorah Housing Foundation, and as a member of the Corporate Fund for Housing. He is also a founder of both the Museum of Contemporary Art and on the board of The Music Center of Los Angeles County.

STANLEY BLACK

Stanley Black is an American real estate investor and philanthropist from Beverly Hills, California. He is the founder and chairman of the Black Equities Group. Through his company, he is the owner of 18 million square feet of commercial real estate in thirty-five states. He is a large supporter of Jewish charities and the Children's Hospital of Los Angeles.

JEFF ELOWE

Jeff Elowe founded The Laramar Group in 2001 after

co-founding Elkor Realty Corp. and Elkor Properties in 1989. As CEO of The Laramar Group, Mr. Elowe oversees an institutional real estate portfolio valued in excess of $2.5 billion. Laramar is a nationally recognized investment and property management firm that has been ranked in the top fifty largest firms in the U.S. by the National Multi-Housing Council. Mr. Elowe is chairman of the investment committee and is responsible for the company's overall strategic planning, investments, asset management, and investor relations. Mr. Elowe has built a successful thirty-year real estate investment track record having sponsored and participated in transactions totaling in excess of $6 billion.

BOB HART

Real estate investment industry veteran Robert E. Hart is the Founder, Chief Executive, and President of TruAmerica Multifamily, which has rapidly become one the nation's largest, most-active and premier investors in apartment communities, with over $8 billion of assets under management totaling approximately 40,000 units.

His three decades of real estate experience includes key executive positions at various national and global real estate investment platforms, where he has overseen the successful acquisition and disposition of more than $12 billion in property assets. Hart is a sought-after interview by leading publications, and has been featured in The

Wall Street Journal, Bloomberg, The Los Angeles Times, and innumerable industry and trade media outlets for his insights into the real estate markets.

MICHAEL SOROCHINSKY

As Founder and Chief Executive Officer of Cypress Equity Investments, Michael Sorochinsky is the visionary of CEI and the driving force behind the company's $5 billion real estate portfolio. Michael's investment strategies, business philosophy, and transaction execution diligence has brought about substantial annualized returns to equity.

In 2010, Michael saw an opportunity to build Class A apartments in top cities around the US and led CEI to amass a development pipeline of over 9,000 luxury apartments with projected value in excess of $5 billion in ten top markets.

ABOUT THE AUTHOR

BRENT SPRENKLE has two decades of commercial real estate experience specializing in the Greater Los Angeles multifamily market. Brent has sold over $1 billion worth of multifamily properties since the start of his career with Sperry Van Ness, Hendricks & Partners and Berkadia. Brent has also purchased and repositioned over twenty properties either on his own or with partners, from apartment buildings, office, industrial, and retail. Brent lives in Manhattan Beach, California, with his wife and four children.